EAC GUIDELINES FOR THE USE OF GEOPHYSICS IN ARCHAEOLOGY

Questions to Ask and Points to Consider

EAC GUIDELINES 2

Armin Schmidt, Paul Linford, Neil Linford, Andrew David,
Chris Gaffney, Apostolos Sarris and Jörg Fassbinder

EXECUTIVE SUMMARY

The aim of these guidelines is to provide an overview of the issues to be considered when undertaking or commissioning geophysical survey in archaeology. As every project differs in its requirements (e.g. from finding sites to creating detailed maps of individual structures) and variations in geological and environmental conditions lead to different geophysical responses, there is no single 'best' survey technique or methodology. This guide, in its European approach, highlights the various questions to be asked before a survey is undertaken. It does not provide recipe-book advice on how to do a geophysical survey or a tick list of which technique is suitable under what conditions: there is no substitute for consulting experienced archaeological geophysicists on these matters. Using geophysical techniques and methods inappropriately will lead to disappointment and may, ultimately, result in archaeologists not using them at all.

There is no formalised standard for the conduct of geophysical survey in archaeology, mainly because there are many parameters that determine the outcome, and there are various purposes for which the results may be used. A variety of geophysical **techniques** is available (e.g. magnetometer, earth resistance and ground penetrating radar (GPR) survey) and an archaeological geophysicist will chose a particular **methodology** for collecting data with any of these techniques (e.g. a gridded survey with a specific transect separation). The choices will depend on the archaeological questions being asked (whether broad, like "are there any archaeological features in this planned road corridor?" or detailed as in "is this wall foundation one brick wide or two?"). The following sections discuss the issues for consideration when selecting geophysical techniques and methodologies, but do not specify specific requirements as these will vary according to context.

PREFACE

These guidelines provide an overview of the issues to be considered when undertaking or commissioning geophysical survey in archaeology. As every project differs in its requirements (e.g. from finding sites to creating detailed maps of individual structures) and variations in geological and environmental conditions lead to different geophysical responses, there is no single 'best' survey technique or methodology. This guide, in its European approach, highlights the various questions to be asked before a survey is undertaken. It does not provide recipe-book advice on how to do a geophysical survey or a tick list of which technique is suitable under what conditions. Experienced archaeological geophysicists should be consulted to address the questions that are being posed. Using geophysical techniques and methods inappropriately will lead to disappointment and may, ultimately, result in archaeologists not using them at all. "If all you have is a hammer (or magnetometer), driving a screw becomes impossible".

Especially in the American literature the term 'remote sensing' is often used to describe geophysical as well as air and space based exploration of underground features (e.g. Wiseman and El-Baz 2007). By contrast, and in line with European traditions, a clear distinction is made here between ground-based geophysical techniques and remote sensing techniques. This is based on the imaging principles underlying the respective technologies. Ground based systems usually collect one spatially registered data sample from each sensor location (e.g. a single reading for each magnetometer, or a single trace from each GPR antenna). Remote sensing techniques, by contrast, collect spatially resolved data from a whole area of investigation from each sensor location, using either the system's optical aperture (e.g. photography) or a scanning device (e.g. laser sampling).

These guidelines are based on the experience of the authors in archaeological geophysics and influenced by various published sources. The bulk of the text is derived from the English Heritage guidelines on *Geophysical Survey* in *Archaeological Field Evaluation* (English Heritage 2008) with terminology modified with reference to other publications (Gaffney and Gater 2003; Schmidt 2013a; Aspinall *et al.* 2008; Schmidt 2013b). The notation of numerical values follows the Anglo-Saxon system whereby the 'decimal point' is represented by a dot.

These guidelines were commissioned by the European Archaeological Council (EAC) and provide information on archaeological geophysics that is generically applicable. There are also some country-specific guidelines in place and additional information may be found in national heritage legislation. Some of this is summarised in a Wiki at www.archprospection.org/eacguidelines, which is continuously being updated.

Geophysical survey for archaeology has a wider academic and professional forum than was the case several years ago. A succession of biennial *International Conferences on Archaeological Prospection* started in 1995 at the University of Bradford in the U.K. and were held subsequently in Japan, Germany, Austria, Poland, Italy, Slovakia, France and Turkey. These meetings were attended by an ever greater variety of specialists in geophysics and remote sensing. The Near Surface Geophysics Group (NSGG) of the Geological Society in Britain has similarly hosted a continuing series of biennial one-day meetings devoted to recent research in the subject and other conference series also include regular sessions on archaeological geophysics (EAGE Near Surface Geoscience, EGU General Assembly, International Conference on GPR etc.). The journal *Archaeological Prospection*, initiated in 1994, has established itself as the main outlet for publication of relevant research and case studies; and the International Society for Archaeological Prospection (ISAP) was formed in 2003 (www.archprospection.org), publishing results from across the world in its quarterly newsletter. Archaeological geophysics is now a component of undergraduate teaching in many countries although currently the only post-graduate degree course specifically devoted to the subject is the MSc in Archaeological Prospection at the University of Bradford (bit.ly/146M4FQ).

CONTENTS

PART I: GUIDANCE FOR GEOPHYSICAL SURVEY — 9
1. INTRODUCTION — 9
2. JUSTIFICATION FOR SURVEY — 10
3. FIELDWORK — 10
    3.1 SURVEY PURPOSE — 10
    3.2 THE SURVEY GRID — 11
    3.3 GROUND COVERAGE — 11
    3.4 SPATIAL RESOLUTION — 12
    3.5 MAGNETOMETER SURVEY — 13
    3.6 EARTH RESISTANCE AREA SURVEY — 13
    3.7 ELECTRICAL RESISTIVITY IMAGING (ERI) — 14
    3.8 GROUND PENETRATING RADAR (GPR) SURVEY — 14
    3.9 LOW FREQUENCY ELECTROMAGNETIC (LFEM) SURVEY — 15
    3.10 MAGNETIC SUSCEPTIBILITY SURVEY — 15
4. DATA TREATMENT — 16
5. DATA INTERPRETATION — 16
6. THE SURVEY REPORT — 17
    6.1 REPORT STRUCTURE AND CONTENTS — 17
    6.2 DATA PRESENTATION – PLOTS AND PLANS — 18
7. DISSEMINATION — 18
8. DATA ARCHIVING — 19
9. COMPETENCE OF SURVEY PERSONNEL — 19

PART II: GEOPHYSICAL SURVEY AND PLANNING APPLICATIONS — 21
1. ARCHAEOLOGY AND PLANNING APPLICATIONS — 21
    1.1 START-UP AND PLANNING — 21
    1.2 EXECUTION — 22
    1.3 CLOSURE — 25
2. BRIEFS AND SPECIFICATIONS — 25
    2.1 THE BRIEF — 26
    2.2 THE SPECIFICATION — 27

CONTENTS

3. THE SURVEY REPORT		29
3.1 SUMMARY		30
3.2 INTRODUCTION		30
3.3 METHODS (TECHNIQUES AND METHODOLOGIES)		31
3.4 RESULTS		31
3.5 CONCLUSIONS		32
3.6 SITE LOCATION PLANS		32
3.7 DATA PRESENTATION – PLOTS AND PLANS		32
3.8 PLOTS OF MINIMALLY ENHANCED DATA		33
3.9 PLOTS OF IMPROVED DATA		34
3.10 PLOTS OF PROCESSED DATA		34
3.11 INTERPRETATIVE DIAGRAMS		34
4. DISSEMINATION		35
4.1 SOURCES OF INFORMATION		35
4.2 DISSEMINATION REQUIREMENTS		36
5. DATA ARCHIVING		36
6. LEGAL CONSIDERATIONS		38
6.1 SITE ACCESS		39
6.2 METAL DETECTORS		39
6.3 GEOPHYSICAL SURVEY		39
PART III: CHOICE OF GEOPHYSICAL TECHNIQUE		**41**
1. INTRODUCTION		41
1.1 EXPECTED MATERIAL CONTRAST		41
1.2 SURVEY PURPOSE		42
1.3 EXPECTED ARCHAEOLOGICAL FEATURES		42
1.4 LOGISTICAL CONSIDERATIONS		42
2. CHOICE OF GEOPHYSICAL SURVEY		42
3. COSTS		43
4. URBAN AND BROWNFIELD SITES		44
5. CEMETERIES		44
6. ALLUVIUM		45
7. WETLANDS		48

8. ROAD AND PIPELINE CORRIDORS	48
9. WIND FARMS	50
10. VERY LARGE AREAS	51

PART IV: INTRODUCTION TO ARCHAEOLOGICAL GEOPHYSICS — 55

1. APPLICATION OF TECHNIQUES — 55
    1.1 THE SURVEY GRID — 55
    1.2 MAGNETOMETER SURVEY — 59
    1.3 EARTH RESISTANCE SURVEY — 67
    1.4 GROUND PENETRATING RADAR — 77
    1.5 LOW-FREQUENCY ELECTROMAGNETIC METHODS — 89
    1.6 TOPSOIL MAGNETIC SUSCEPTIBILITY SURVEY — 91
    1.7 OTHER GEOPHYSICAL METHODS — 93
    1.8 METAL DETECTING — 98
    1.9 GEOCHEMICAL METHODS — 100

2. ANALYSIS OF GEOPHYSICAL DATA — 100
    2.1 DATA TREATMENT — 100
    2.2 DATA DISPLAY — 109
    2.3 DATA INTERPRETATION — 116

PART V: REFERENCES — 119

PART VI: APPENDICES — 129

1. GLOSSARY — 129
2. RELATED STANDARDS, CODES AND GUIDANCE — 133
3. EDITORIAL INFORMATION — 135
    3.1 CONTRIBUTORS — 135
    3.2 LIST OF PEOPLE CONSULTED — 135

LIST OF FIGURES

Figure 1: The GEEP towed mobile sensor platform with built-in GPS.	57
Figure 2: Field trial data collected at Wroxeter Roman city using the GEEP system.	58
Figure 3: Handheld magnetometer systems.	59
Figure 4: Cart mounted magnetometer systems.	60
Figure 5: Greyscale plots of caesium (a) and fluxgate (b) gradiometer data.	61
Figure 6: Caesium magnetometer and fluxgate gradiometer data collected at varying sample intervals.	65
Figure 7: Caesium magnetometer (a) and earth resistance (b) survey of the same area.	69
Figure 8: Earth resistance devices in use.	70
Figure 9: Earth resistance survey conducted using six different electrode separations.	71
Figure 10: Earth resistance surveys at Freens Court, Herefordshire; comparison of sampling density.	72
Figure 11: Earth resistance surveys over the same area at Stanwick Roman Villa, Northamptonshire repeated at monthly intervals for eighteen months.	73
Figure 12: Earth resistance survey at Basing House, Hampshire.	75
Figure 13: Annotated photograph of a Sensors and Software Pulse Ekko 1000 GPR system.	79
Figure 14: The vertical and horizontal resolution of a GPR system are determined by the antenna.	81
Figure 15: Trial GPR transect collected over peaty soil repeated with 450MHz (a) and 225MHz (b) centre frequency antennas.	83
Figure 16: Examples of modes of display for three-dimensional GPR data.	85
Figure 17: An estimate of the average subsurface velocity (v) can be obtained by conducting a common mid-point (CMP) survey in the field.	87
Figure 18: Compact EM instruments with an inter-coil separation of 1m are well suited to archaeological surveys.	90
Figure 19: Comparison between different survey techniques over a buried Roman wall.	91
Figure 20: Area magnetic susceptibility survey.	92
Figure 21: Bartington MS2 magnetic susceptibility meter in use.	93
Figure 22: Systematic metal detector survey of an area that has been divided into 10 m grid cells.	99
Figure 23: Common corrections for magnetometer data.	102
Figure 24: Earth resistance data over a long barrow.	106
Figure 25: Inversion of an electrical section over a ditch.	108
Figure 26: Different trace plot displays.	109
Figure 27: Colour contour plots.	111
Figure 28: Different display options for magnetometer data.	113
Figure 29: Three-dimensional representations of geophysical data.	115

LIST OF TABLES

Table 1: Examples of effective spatial resolution	12
Table 2: Summary of expected GPR response over various types of sites and features.	76
Table 3: Approximate values for the variation of GPR penetration depth and resolution with centre frequency	80
Table 4: Factors that may effect the data	117

PART I: GUIDANCE FOR GEOPHYSICAL SURVEY

1. INTRODUCTION

There is no formalised standard for the conduct of geophysical survey in archaeology, mainly because there are many parameters that determine the outcome, and there are various purposes for which the results may be used. A variety of geophysical **techniques** is available (e.g. magnetometer, earth resistance and ground penetrating radar (GPR) survey) and an archaeological geophysicist will chose a particular **methodology** for collecting data with any of these techniques (e.g. a gridded survey with a specific transect separation). The choices will be made according to the archaeological questions being posed (whether broad as in "are there any archaeological features in this planned road corridor?" or detailed, like "is this wall foundation one brick wide or two?").

One approach to selecting appropriate survey parameters (techniques and methodologies) is to collate regional experiences, either listing types of features (e.g. hearths) against suitable techniques (e.g. magnetometer area survey) (e.g. English Heritage 2008, Table 3) or in the form of software decision tools (Somers *et al.* 2003). However such tools are necessarily empirical and usually applicable to only a narrow range of conditions. There is a danger that archaeological features may be entirely missed through over-prescriptive adherence to their 'standard' recommendations under inappropriate circumstances (e.g. use of magnetometer area survey for the investigation of non-magnetic wall footings, just because its is listed in a table; using a 1 m traverse separation when looking for 0.2 m wide post holes). Hence a different approach is presented here. The following sections lay out the issues to be considered when selecting geophysical techniques and methodologies, rather than detailing specific requirements that would certainly not be appropriate in all possible conditions and in all countries.

In these guidelines Part II (Geophysical Survey and Planning Applications) and Part III (Guide to Choice of Methods) are mainly aimed at those who commission surveys while Part IV is a more in-depth description and assessment of the main techniques and methodologies for those more concerned with these. Although the latter goes beyond the remit of 'guidelines', this Part serves as a useful reference as it expands on some of the issues mentioned in Parts I to III.

It is expected that the commissioning and undertaking of geophysical surveys in archaeology will be carried out in accordance with national and international professional standards and legal requirements. The legal context will vary from country to country and practitioners always need to make themselves aware of relevant legal requirements.

2. JUSTIFICATION FOR SURVEY

Prior to fieldwork, it is good practice that the geophysical survey requirements be integrated within a written statement (the 'project design', 'specification', 'written scheme of investigation', or 'survey contract'). This should include an explicit justification for the choice of survey techniques and methodologies, while allowing some flexibility if modification in the light of particular site conditions at the time of fieldwork is required. The choices of survey techniques and methodologies will be appropriately matched with the archaeological and logistical demands of the project. The written statement should also contain a list of deliverables of the survey (e.g. survey report, data in a specific format, ownership of intellectual property rights). This is stressed to ensure that all parties to a survey project understand their commitments and what can be delivered.

3. FIELDWORK

All fieldwork should be conducted under the principle of repeatability; in other words, that, within reason, it should be possible for independent re-measurement of the results[1].

Fieldworkers must ensure that every effort is made on site to be courteous and considerate in their dealings with landowners, local residents and organisations, respecting all aspects of the environment. A high level of professionalism is necessary at all times.

Correct observance must be made of any legal constraints on sites, for example obtaining official permission for undertaking geophysical survey in general, for which many countries have enacted national legislation that reflects the 1992 Valetta Treaty (Council of Europe 1992; bit.ly/136czi7). In some countries sites that were given particular protection status require specific permits (for example in the U.K. by obtaining a 'Section 42 Licence' for survey over scheduled monuments, or in Italy and Greece by obtaining a permit from the Ministry of Culture). The relevant regional or national heritage bodies should always be consulted if in doubt. It is important to remember that there may also be non-archaeological constraints (e.g. ecological or environmental) that need to be observed.

3.1 SURVEY PURPOSE

The purpose of a survey should be established at the outset so that appropriate geophysical techniques and survey methodologies can be chosen. Whether the precise shape of postholes of approximately 0.2 m size is required or the location of a 2 m wide brick kiln makes a big difference in terms of spatial resolution and sensitivity of the instruments selected. A useful categorisation is provided by Gaffney & Gater (2003), who distinguish three broad levels of investigation.

---

[1] Notwithstanding changes due to altered environmental conditions.

- Level 1 – Prospection: to identify areas of archaeological potential and individual strong anomalies.
- Level 2 – Delineation: to delimit and map archaeological sites and features.
- Level 3 – Characterisation: to analyse in detail the shape of individual anomalies.

3.2 THE SURVEY GRID

The survey grid is the network of control points used to locate the geophysical survey measurements relative to base mapping or to absolute positions on the Earth's surface (see Part IV, 1.1). Whether physically marked on the ground or measured during survey using a global positioning system (GPS/GNSS), these should be located on the ground to survey-grade accuracy (±0.1 m). To allow the geophysical data to be used as part of the national archaeological site archive the survey grid should be independently re-locatable on the ground by a third party, by measurement to local permanent features, and/or by the use of GPS/GNSS coordinates. For GPS/GNSS measurements the possible difference between an instrument's precision (e.g. 0.05 m) and the overall locational accuracy of the data (e.g. 5 m with respect to a national grid system) has to be considered carefully. For example RTK-GPS measurements without a known passive GPS station ('GPS-Trig Point') may have a very high precision (e.g. 0.01 m), but the absolute accuracy is sometimes only around 5 m, dependent on the fix of the base station. National GPS/GNSS networks (e.g. SmartNet (www.smartnet-eu.com), the commercial Trimble-VRS network available in many European countries (http://bit.ly/1h9e4Ax) or OS Net (bit.ly/1jUqPRY) in the U.K.) usually provide the highest accuracy as they are based on accurately known reference points. Similarly, fully post-processed RTK-GPS measurements may also achieve an accuracy that matches this precision.

All locational information must be geo-referenced and annotated with the geographic coordinate system used (e.g. WGS84, UTM-WGS84 or National Grid). It is strongly recommended to use the same coordinate system for the locational information that will later be used for the presentation of the geophysical data, as conversion between them may introduce inaccuracies. Since curved coordinate systems (e.g. WGS84 lat./lon.) are less suited for the presentation of planar geophysical data they are not usually recommended for the accurate recording of locational information.

In certain cases (e.g. where permanent features are absent), and with appropriate permission, it may be acceptable to emplace permanent survey markers. Care should be taken to ensure that any survey markers or other equipment is not a hazard to people or animals.

3.3 GROUND COVERAGE

Full coverage of a site is always the preferred option, since incomplete data-sets resulting from a sampling strategy may seriously limit the archaeological interpretation of the detected geophysical anomalies (Gaffney and Gater 2003). In addition, as with any archaeological sampling strategy, individual features or small sites may be missed entirely.

However, for Level 1 investigations (Prospection) the total extent of a scheme may exceed the area that can be reasonably surveyed in its entirety (see Part III, 10). If a sampling strategy is chosen, it should cover at least 50% of the total area with geophysical survey. It is advisable to lay out the rationale of a sampling strategy in advance and discuss it with the survey team as the logistics of implementing an elaborate scheme may eliminate the perceived cost savings.

3.4 SPATIAL RESOLUTION

The spatial resolution of a geophysical survey relates to the size of archaeological features[2] that are expected, or are searched for, and the level of detail that is required (see Section 3.1, Survey purpose). For gridded surveys the area of investigation is subdivided into small rectangular cells, forming a measurement raster (e.g. 0.25 m by 1.0 m). The dimensions of these measurement cells determine the resolution of a survey in its two orthogonal directions (x and y, or Easting and Northing). Data are usually collected along transects so that the sampling interval along transects (usually referred to as x-resolution or in-line resolution) and the line separation (the y-resolution or cross-line resolution)[3] describe the two survey resolutions. For the purpose of detecting and characterising subsurface features it was shown (Schmidt and Marshall 1997) that the resolving power of a survey is mostly determined by the coarser of these two resolutions, which is usually the line separation. A useful estimate is the '**effective spatial resolution**' of a survey. It can be defined as the *larger* of the x- and y-resolution, but reduced down to 2/3 of this, if the orthogonal resolution is correspondingly smaller[4]. Table 1 shows some examples to illustrate this measure. The effective spatial resolution should be matched to the detail and size of features that are to be investigated. Similarly, the depth resolution of vertical imaging techniques needs to be suitable for the required investigation (e.g. by choosing an appropriate GPR frequency, see Part IV, 1.4.2)

Survey resolution		Effective spatial resolution
1.0 m	× 1.0 m	1.00 m
0.5 m	× 1.0 m	0.67 m
0.125 m	× 1.0 m	0.67 m
0.5 m	× 0.5 m	0.50 m
0.25 m	× 0.5 m	0.33 m

Table 1: Examples of effective spatial resolution.

If an un-gridded survey is undertaken (e.g. with a magnetometer linked to a GPS/GNSS or a towed earth resistance array) similar considerations apply. The same spatial resolution should be maintained throughout the survey area by using a guidance system to follow

---

[2] Strictly speaking, the size of the anomaly of the archaeological features is the relevant measure.
[3] A single survey transect may record several lines of data simultaneously, for example with a two-sensor magnetometer.
[4] effective resolution = $\min(\Delta y, \max(2/3 * \Delta y, \Delta x))$

equally spaced transects or another methodology with similar outcome. Uneven spatial data density, for example due to entirely random data collection or uneven speed of acquisition, may create biases during data interpretation and should be avoided.

3.5 MAGNETOMETER SURVEY

For a Level 1 investigation (Prospection), and some Level 2 investigations (Delineation) a survey resolution not coarser than 1.0 m × 0.25 m has previously been recommended (English Heritage 2008). However, for the analysis of individual features (Level 2 - Delineation or Level 3 - Characterisation) a higher resolution is required, for instance 0.25 m × 0.25 m for the characterisation of individual pits, and 0.5 m × 0.25 m is a good compromise for most investigations. Since magnetometer surveys measure the existing magnetic field (passive method) any denser sampling will reveal more detail. In order to achieve the required sampling density a continuously recording magnetometer should be used. It must have sufficient sensitivity to detect clearly the anomalies created by the features concerned.

Area survey is the preferred method of ground coverage in all instances. Magnetometer scanning[5] is discouraged as a survey technique as its results cannot normally be reproduced. It may however be used to gain an overview of the magnetic responses of a site so that an appropriate evaluation strategy can be developed for the subsequent use of other techniques. Magnetometer scanning should not otherwise be included in briefs or specifications and certainly not used as a sole investigation method.

3.6 EARTH RESISTANCE AREA SURVEY

The maximum acceptable survey resolution for earth resistance area surveys is 1 m × 1 m. Since earth resistance methods sample a volume of ground that is determined by the electrode separation[6] a survey resolution that is smaller than the electrode separation only improves marginally the spatial information content of the results (Schmidt 2013a).

Area surveys using the twin-probe or square/trapezoidal array electrode configuration are the preferred methods of ground coverage. Other methods require special justification in the survey design.

For twin-probe systems in archaeological survey the mobile electrode separation should usually be 0.5 m; wider separations require justification. The equivalent dimension for a square array would typically be 0.75 m.

---

[5] Magnetometer scanning is the practice whereby an operator walks across the survey area and marks positions where the magnetometer displays particularly high readings.
[6] Since earth resistance survey is an active method (i.e. generating its own signal) the survey resolution is limited by the size of the electrode array used. The measured data are a convolution of the signal from the buried feature with the spatial characteristics of the device.

3.7 ELECTRICAL RESISTIVITY IMAGING (ERI)

Electrical resistivity imaging (ERI) is usually undertaken with two-dimensional electrode layouts (i.e. along lines) or with mobile multiplexed electrode arrays. Several parallel two-dimensional data-sets can be combined after the survey to form three-dimensional data volumes. The smallest electrode separation used should reflect the size of the features sought and the shallowest depth where they may be found. For typical archaeological features it should not be larger than 1 m and it has been found that an electrode separation of 0.5 m is very beneficial for the archaeological interpretation of results.

If a switched device is used that collects measurements with several different electrode configurations (electrical resistivity tomography, ERT) appropriate software is required to analyse these data, usually applying inversion. By arranging the electrodes in a two-dimensional pattern on the surface instead of using individual survey lines results can be improved even further (Papadopoulos *et al.* 2006).

3.8 GROUND PENETRATING RADAR (GPR) SURVEY

Generally, this technique is used for detailed investigations of a site to create time slices, depth maps or volume renderings of buried anomalies. Using only an isolated profile is not well suited for archaeological interpretations and should only be considered where large linear soil features are expected and crossed at right angles (e.g. moats, wide ditches).

To create a three-dimensional data cube (two horizontal spatial dimensions, and the travel-time of the signal) from which the time slices can be derived, measurements are usually collected along several parallel linear transects and resampled along the transects to form a regular grid. If an un-gridded survey is undertaken data processing will have to take possible changes of antenna directions into account and 3D data interpolation requires special considerations.

Data can be collected with single antennas or antenna arrays. The footprint of a GPR antenna depends mainly on its frequency, increasing with the depth of investigation (see Part IV, 1.4.2) and for typical archaeological applications at shallow depth is often in the order of 0.2-0.5 m. The effective spatial resolution should be similar to the footprint and a line separation of 0.25 m is usually required to visualise the shape of buried archaeological features. If the shape is of lesser importance a line separation of 0.5 m may be acceptable. Along each transect data should be collected at close intervals of approximately 0.05 m to allow for appropriate data processing.

Specific site conditions, choice of antenna or the aims of the survey may require an alternative sampling methodology, but this should be justified in the supporting specification documents.

The choice of the antenna's centre frequency will be based on the expected size and depth of archaeological features (see Part IV, 1.4.2) and the estimated signal loss (usually strong attenuation in wet or salty soils). It is advisable to undertake field tests prior to the selection of antenna frequency and survey resolution, and provisions should be made in a brief for adjusting the final survey parameters.

During fieldwork some provision should be made for determining the electromagnetic ground velocity so that measured signal travel-times can be converted to depths. If sufficient reflection hyperbolas are found in the data, these may be used, but otherwise calibration with features at known depth, or common midpoint (CMP) antenna spreads may be necessary. Information about the variation of electromagnetic velocity will also allow generating horizontal depth slices.

3.9 LOW FREQUENCY ELECTROMAGNETIC (LFEM) SURVEY

Low frequency electromagnetic survey (LFEM[7]), which collects in-phase and quadrature electromagnetic signals (usually labelled as magnetic susceptibility and conductivity, respectively) is similar in its methodology to magnetometer survey and the same methodology-guidelines apply. However, since LFEM is an active method, reducing the survey resolution below the instrument's measurement envelope does not improve the data noticeably. The measurement envelope can be estimated for most applications as one-third of the instrument size (the coil separation of a Slingram device, or the coil size of a time-domain device). This size also determines for most soils the depth of penetration and should be selected according to the size and depth of expected features. Modern instruments can collect data for different coil separations and orientations simultaneously and thereby provide information about soil properties at different depths (De Smedt *et al.* 2013b).

3.10 MAGNETIC SUSCEPTIBILITY SURVEY

Magnetic susceptibility surveys are traditionally undertaken by collecting soil samples with a coarse survey resolution for subsequent magnetic susceptibility measurements in the laboratory. If LFEM instruments (either in the form of Slingram devices or as specific magnetic susceptibility field coils) are used to measure magnetic susceptibility *in situ* with similarly coarse sampling resolutions these are also referred to as magnetic susceptibility survey.

In favourable conditions magnetic susceptibility survey can highlight areas of increased human impact, but whether there is a causal link between high readings and past anthropogenic activities is not always clear. Undertaking magnetometer survey over the areas of high magnetic susceptibility and over some areas of low magnetic susceptibility is therefore advisable to form an understanding of the underlying features. Magnetic susceptibility survey is not a substitute for magnetometer survey.

---

[7] Sometimes also referred to as Electromagnetic Induction (EMI) survey.

Although agricultural activities may spread out soil with enhanced magnetic susceptibility, a maximum survey resolution of 5 m is recommended. For a coarse Level 1 investigation (Prospection) this may be increased to 10 m. Un-gridded surveys are also possible but should retain a similar effective spatial resolution. In addition to the investigation of topsoil magnetic susceptibility (either by sampling or through LFEM measurements) it is advisable to collect some measurements from subsoil and local archaeological features to draw comparisons that will help in analysing the data.

4. DATA TREATMENT

It is advisable that area surveys are conducted, and data subsequently treated, to produce a data-set that is as uniform as possible. Instruments should be set up carefully and measurements collected with the highest possible quality to minimise the need for subsequent data treatment, as this can introduce artefacts in the results. For example stripes in survey data and mismatches between data grids should be avoided.

A copy of unprocessed raw data must be retained and archived for quality control and to allow further processing if needed (see Part II, 5).

Data-collection artefacts apparent in the survey data should be identified and removed using appropriate data treatment (Data-Improvement stage, see also Part IV, 2.1). All such processing should be documented clearly. Data-collection artefacts that cannot be corrected computationally should be described and distinguished from possible archaeological anomalies. If the data have been seriously compromised during collection, a return to the site to re-survey the affected areas should be considered.

To highlight relevant anomalies in a survey for readers of the resulting report further data treatment may be necessary (e.g. filtering during the Data Processing stage). Such data processing has to be described in the documentation and the possible side effects highlighted (e.g. during high-pass filtering processing artefacts may be introduced and the size of anomalies often changes).

5. DATA INTERPRETATION

It is recommended that the archaeological interpretation of survey data is undertaken by competent archaeological geophysicists (see Section 9, Competence of survey personnel) who are knowledgeable about the geophysical characteristics of the data, and the archaeological and geomorphological conditions prevailing on site. Consultation should also take place with other site specialists (e.g. landscape archaeologists, aerial photographers) or their reports, wherever possible.

The interpretation of magnetometer and magnetic susceptibility data should try to distinguish anthropogenic from other causes of magnetic enhancement.

A clear distinction must always be made between interpretation that is scientifically demonstrable, and interpretation based on informed speculation. The attribution of anomalies to predefined classes of features needs to be documented in detail (see Part IV, 2.3).

Geophysical data cannot be used as 'negative evidence', since the lack of geophysical anomalies cannot be taken to imply a lack of archaeological features. However, where a corpus of previous work is available for the same environmental and geological conditions a statistical probability for the existence of archaeological features may be derived from the geophysical data, taking the resolving power of the used methodology into account. Such estimates have to be fully qualified and explained. Where decisions have to be made in the absence of geophysical anomalies an additional evaluation procedure – for instance the use of a different geophysical technique, or trial trenching – should be considered.

6. THE SURVEY REPORT

All fieldwork must be followed by a report. This will be a clear and succinct text, supported by tables, figures, appendices and references as necessary. It ought to stand independent of supporting material and should combine the qualities of concise technical description linked to lucid and objective analysis and interpretation. It is desirable that in the most part it is intelligible to specialists and non-specialists alike. It should usually be accompanied by a statement of the authors' and contractors' professional qualifications.

6.1 REPORT STRUCTURE AND CONTENTS

The report will normally contain the following elements:

- title page;
- summary of results;
- introduction;
- methods (techniques and methodologies);
- results;
- conclusions;
- acknowledgements;
- statement of indemnity;
- references; and
- appendices.

Further detail on reports is provided in Part II, 3.

6.2 DATA PRESENTATION – PLOTS AND PLANS

Depending on the geophysical methods used, each report should include:

- a survey location plan demonstrating relationships to other mapped features and indicating the position of individual data grids (minimum scale 1:2500);
- a greyscale plot of minimally enhanced survey data, for example using only grid balancing/edge matching (see Part IV, 2.2 ; preferred minimum scale 1:1000);
- a greyscale plot of improved survey data (see Part IV, 2.1.1; minimum scale 1:1000);
- a greyscale plot of processed survey data (see Part IV, 2.1.2; minimum scale 1:1000);
- where appropriate (see Part IV, 2.2) a X-Y trace plot of improved magnetic data (for large sites a sample of the data might be plotted instead, to support the specific interpretation of anomalies identified from greyscale images); and
- one or more interpretative plans/diagrams (minimum scale 1:1000).

The survey location plan should show national grid coordinates to be directly relatable to the official national map base, where this is available and reliable. In other cases alternative map products may be used. In all instances the copyright restrictions of the map data have to be observed and due acknowledgement given to their source.

Each plan and/or plot must have a scale-bar or annotated metric grid and an accurately oriented north arrow. The plot (or text in the report) will specify 'which north' this arrow indicates (usually grid north, but possibly magnetic or geographic north).

Greyscale and trace (X–Y) plots must also have a range-bar, annotated with values and units, indicating the range of the variable depicted.

For 'vertical' data plots the scale of both axes (x- and y-axis) has to be indicated. For GPR profiles the vertical scale is usually the two-way travel time. If an estimated depth scale is also included, there must be an explanation of how it was derived (see Part IV, 1.4.5). For ERI profiles the vertical scale may be a pseudo-depth derived from the electrode separation (pseudosection). If an inverted resistivity section is shown the parameters of the inversion must be provided. If the ground level is significantly uneven (e.g. ±0.5 m over 5 m) along the survey traverse concerned, a topographically corrected section should be considered.

Legends must be provided that describe the symbols and conventions used.

7. DISSEMINATION

A copy of the survey report (paper and/or digital, as required) should be lodged with the relevant national, and where applicable regional, heritage organisation and responsibility for this must be attributed clearly to either the contractor or the commissioning body at the outset of the work.

8. DATA ARCHIVING

A minimum requirement is that a viable digital Archive of the survey should be retained for future interrogation (Schmidt 2013b). This usually comprises (i) the raw and processed data in their original, possibly proprietary, format (Working Files), (ii) a version of the raw data in a format that can be maintained easily and read by most software (Preservation Files, for example 'xyz text files'), (iii) image files that represent these data, (iv) the report, (v) a brief description of all files in the Archive and (vi) metadata that list the survey techniques and methodologies (e.g. sampling intervals), project and site information and georeferencing. A detailed list of possible metadata is provided by Schmidt (2013b), but subsets may be sufficient (e.g. OASIS data fields in the U.K.). Additional national requirements must be observed.

This Archive should be deposited with an Archiving Body to preserve the data. Whether this is the survey contractor, a cloud storage provider or a national archiving organisation should be specified at the outset of the work, together with any confidentiality considerations. Sufficient resources for the compilation of the Archive and its deposition to an Archiving Body must be allocated.

If the commissioning body (or another organisation) requires to hold the intellectual property rights (IPRs) in the data a transfer needs to be arranged, as in most cases the IPRs are initially held by the individuals who carried out the survey, or their employer if it was undertaken as part of their employment. As the data may have monetary value such a transfer is specified preferably at the outset of the work.

9. COMPETENCE OF SURVEY PERSONNEL

All staff, including sub-contractors, should be suitably qualified and competent for their respective project roles. It is important that fieldwork staff have received training to operate equipment in such a way that data of the highest quality are collected. Archaeological geophysicists will have experience in applying geophysical survey in an archaeological context and have some understanding of the geophysical principles and archaeological requirements. They may have been trained at University (at undergraduate, postgraduate or doctoral level in archaeology and/or an appropriate science) or as part of their employment.

In particular, the project manager of an archaeological geophysical survey is recommended to have:

- competence in basic metric survey procedure;
- extended experience in geophysical survey in archaeology (including fieldwork, data processing, data interpretation and reporting) in a supervised capacity; and

- evidence of relevant formal training (academic or as part of their employment).

Less experienced staff should be supervised throughout any fieldwork, data treatment, data interpretation, and report preparation.

Membership of national and international professional institutions is encouraged (e.g. *European GPR Association* (EuroGPR)) to keep abreast of current developments and subscribe to professional codes of conduct. The *International Society for Archaeological Prospection* (ISAP) is an international organisation that promotes best practice in archaeological geophysics, and provides a forum for the exchange of results, new technological developments and the potential of geophysical survey in archaeology.

PART II: GEOPHYSICAL SURVEY AND PLANNING APPLICATIONS

1. ARCHAEOLOGY AND PLANNING APPLICATIONS

Many countries have legislation and/or policies in place which have the effect of ensuring that archaeological and cultural heritage assessment is normally part of the planning process that precedes major building or infrastructure developments. For example the U.K. National Planning Policy Framework states *"Where a site on which development is proposed includes or has the potential to include heritage assets with archaeological interest, local planning authorities should require developers to submit an appropriate desk-based assessment and, where necessary, a field evaluation."* (Department for Communities and Local Government 2012, Paragraph 128). In other countries, for example in most states of Germany, only known sites are protected and it is the national heritage departments' responsibility to undertake a preliminary desktop evaluation to establish whether any know site may be affected by a development project. However, since the regulations that apply to the discovery of unknown sites during building work are very stringent, with the potential for substantial costs to the developers, more detailed evaluations are often recommended in advance of a project.

The potential contribution of geophysical survey should be considered in each instance where development is proposed.

As geophysical survey will often be a crucial element in site evaluation it is most important that it should be integrated in briefs and specifications and within subsequent project management geophysical survey should be part of an integrated programme of research. A typical project will often proceed through a number of stages (Lee 2006).

1.1 START-UP AND PLANNING

Consideration of geophysical survey can be most crucial during the early stages of project planning. Indeed, in many programmes of archaeological evaluation the geophysical survey will be completed and acted upon, as a self-contained project, entirely within this phase. In the right circumstances such survey can provide information of great clarity on the extent and nature of archaeological deposits and features. Even in less perfect conditions, survey results can be highly informative, and therefore it is important that geophysical methods should always be considered at the outset of each programme of evaluation.

Most evaluations will be initiated with a desktop study, often starting with an interrogation of the relevant local sites and monuments records, followed by an assessment of all other documentary records, including aerial photographic coverage. In addition, such a study should determine the following information of particular relevance to geophysical survey:

- solid geology;
- drift geology;
- soil type;
- current land use and surface conditions;
- history of previous ground disturbance;
- history of previous geophysical survey (if any); and
- legal status of the site.

Once this information is available, the potential for geophysical survey should be assessed. If geophysical survey is then agreed to be relevant, a project design or specification can be drawn up, calling upon expert advice in order to avoid wasteful or misdirected outlay of resources, or missed opportunities.

1.2 EXECUTION

Project Execution, as defined here, includes fieldwork, assessment of potential, archive deposition, and dissemination (Lee 2006).

1.2.1 Fieldwork
The following stages of geophysical survey fieldwork should be considered and planned for, where appropriate:

- Pilot (test or trial) survey: occasionally it may be necessary for a preliminary assessment to be made of a site's response to geophysical survey, particularly where large areas are concerned. This procedure should indicate whether local conditions are suitable so that useful results can be obtained, and what techniques and methodologies may be most appropriate. Such preliminary information, based on assessment by archaeological geophysicists, can avoid wasting resources on inappropriate techniques and on sites where the use of geophysics is unlikely to be helpful. Sometimes even a brief site visit or site photographs from a client may be all that is required to rule out certain techniques and methodologies. Any pilot survey should not usually take more than a day and the results should be made available immediately for incorporation into the overall project design. The justification for subsequent full geophysical survey should be made clear.
- Full survey: once this justification is assured an agreed survey strategy can be applied. This may be full or partial coverage of the site at high or low levels of detail, using one or more techniques, depending on the strategy adopted.
- Extended coverage: in some circumstances it may be necessary to accommodate additional survey if earlier results (or subsequent excavation) indicate that this would be profitable. Where appropriate, allowance for such contingencies should be made in briefs and specifications.

It is particularly important to establish an agreed timetable for the above stages of survey so that they can be integrated with other evaluation strategies on the site. For example, in some instances survey will take place after field walking, utilising a shared grid system, but before trial trenching or excavation. The timetable should be sufficiently flexible to accommodate additional contingency survey, and costing should allow for this. Above all, the timetable should permit adequate time for the results of geophysical survey to be fully reported in order to inform subsequent project planning.

Once the report has been made available, allowance should be made for the archaeological project team to communicate with the geophysical surveyors to discuss any outstanding matters, especially as these may relate to the archaeological interpretation of the geophysical data.

Good timetabling requires full and informed cooperation between all parties. Particularly relevant to geophysical survey is that landowners and/or their agents and/or tenants have been informed and given their permission for the survey to take place. Obtaining such permissions, as well as details of access and the resolving of any other local complications, should usually be the responsibility of the archaeological project manager rather than that of the geophysical surveyors.

The above recommendations should be followed wherever possible. It is acknowledged, however, that very often practical necessity – particularly shortage of time – may dictate a different course of action. For instance, there may be insufficient time to prepare a full report in advance of excavation or of the development itself, in which case survey plots produced in the field may be used to be acted upon directly.

Once the survey strategy and its projected costs have been agreed, timetabled and the relevant permissions obtained, the fieldwork can go ahead accordingly. Fieldwork procedures are discussed more fully in Part IV.

In the context of the full research programme, geophysical survey will usually be incorporated in the Initiation Stage, allowing its results to influence the subsequent Execution Stage of the larger programme.

1.2.2 Assessment of potential
There are two contexts where assessment of the potential for future use of the geophysical survey data may be required as part of the Execution Stage of the larger programme.

(a) The geophysical data may indicate that further geophysical survey would be of significant advantage to the realisation of archaeological research objectives. There are many instances where extended geophysical survey could significantly enhance the value of a project by placing a partially recorded site within a wider spatial context, in which crucial relationships with other features, sites or the wider landscape can be understood better. This synthetic role of geophysical survey should never be underestimated.

Any such additional survey should be justified and planned for in an updated project design. It should, if possible, employ the original geophysical survey team; if other geophysical surveyors must be used then the archaeological project manager should ensure that full continuity and integration of survey procedure and interpretation is achieved. If at all possible, the original raw field data should be made accessible to the incoming geophysical surveyors.

(b) It is sometimes the case that the geophysical survey data, in their own right, have significant potential for advancing research into geophysical prospecting techniques, or the interpretation of geophysical data. This potential should be assessed throughout a project by the geophysical survey team, and kept under review.

In both cases (a) and (b) above, geophysical survey data have a research potential and should be considered alongside other more customary 'post-excavation' data. If deemed significant and justified by the archaeological project team, any scope for realisation of this potential should be included in an updated project design, for which additional funding will have to be sought. Such a revised project design will include provision for the publication of results either within the main project report, or as a separate paper in a more specialised publication.

1.2.3 Archive deposition
While the full details of the geophysical survey will be archived at the conclusion of the survey project (see Section 5, Data archiving), the project manager and survey staff should be aware of the necessity of recording and safeguarding raw data, the data processing steps undertaken, and locational information, at all appropriate stages during the course of the project.

1.2.4 Dissemination
The results of the main research programme will be drawn up, in draft report form, for review and subsequent publication. However, the report on the geophysical survey will usually have been completed and presented to the project team and/or commissioning body earlier. Close liaison with the project team should continue, however, to ensure that the geophysical data and their interpretation is presented in appropriate proportion to its contribution to the stated objectives of the wider programme.

The following options can be considered for the final presentation of the geophysical survey results:

- that a summary should be included in the main report text, while the survey report and related data are retained in archive;
- that a summary should be included in the main report text, while the survey report is included as an appendix; or
- that the survey report should be modified for reproduction in the main report text.

It is not acceptable for the contribution of geophysical survey to be ignored, even if results have been indifferent or negative. A minimum requirement is that a summary statement is recorded in the overall programme report.

In many countries copyright legislation implies that the organisation or person undertaking fieldwork and reporting results retains the copyright to the material, *unless stated otherwise in the contract* for the work. The actual position should be made clear to all relevant parties at the outset of work by including an explicit copyright statement in any contract.

Every effort should be made to ensure that the survey report becomes publicly accessible. All field data and reports will be deposited with the site archive, and the local historic record office is informed about the outcomes, and possibly presented with a copy of the report and/or data, according to national requirements. Where results for some reason cannot be disclosed, a minimal record should be made and fully updated within a reasonable time. A fuller discussion of dissemination and archiving follows in Sections 4 and 5.

1.3 CLOSURE

Once the survey project has been concluded, time should be planned for documentation of any follow-on actions, unresolved issues and lessons learned.

2. BRIEFS AND SPECIFICATIONS

Definitions of terms used in this section are provided in the glossary, and references can be found in the bibliography. This description of a brief and its further specifications reflects a comprehensive analysis of the information that is required to plan and define a geophysical survey. National guidelines may require different content or organisation of the material. However, it should be considered to include all information listed here, if necessary in an annex. The documentation may need to be adapted to the circumstances of each survey or project.

In a commercial tendering situation, briefs are provided by the client, and tenders invited; tenderers will then respond with a specification or project design. If a tenderer considers a different approach to that identified in the brief to be suited better to the circumstances, then this can be proposed as an alternative specification with separate costs. The final specification or project design will subsequently be agreed with the planning archaeologist or curator, and will form part of a contract that must be drawn up in writing. Even if the geophysical survey is undertaken by a sub-contractor the initial contractual obligations have to be met.

While the time-constraints inherent in a developer-funded scenario are not underestimated, geophysical survey should only be commissioned after careful consideration of the relevant issues discussed in these guidelines. Commissioning survey based on a hasty phone call should be avoided.

2.1 THE BRIEF

A requirement for geophysical survey may become apparent during either the appraisal or the assessment stage in response to an application for development. The earlier this is realised and incorporated into a brief the better. Clients and curators are encouraged to seek specialist advice to ensure that the content of the brief is fully appropriate to the circumstances in each case. If necessary, independent advice on geophysical survey can be sought from independent consultants from outside of the commercial sector.

The following information usually needs to be provided in a brief:

- *Summary*: a concise statement (200 words maximum) of the purpose of the survey, what type of survey is required, by whom, why, where and by when a report must be delivered.
- *Background*: a brief account of the relevant context to the survey requirement. It should include the following:
    - detailed map location(s);
    - designations (e.g. protected monument inventory number);
    - archaeological context (e.g. evidence from aerial photographs, surface remains, documents, known archaeological investigations on the site and in its vicinity);
    - relevant recent history of the site (e.g. landscaping);
    - reasons for the survey; and
    - any wider project context.
- *Site conditions*: a site description, to include the following:
    - underlying solid and drift geology, and soil type(s);
    - likely ground/vegetation conditions at the time of the survey; and
    - ownership and any tenancies in place.
- *Survey location*: a map of a suitable scale to show the context, location and size of the proposed survey area(s).
- *The geophysical survey requirement*: this will state the objectives of the geophysical survey and the techniques by which these are intended to be achieved. The details of the required methodology can either be provided directly in the brief (or its appendix) or in a separate Specification.
- *Timetable*: a statement or tabulation of the project timetable, emphasising the scheduling of fieldwork and report presentation.
- *Further information*: anything further of broad relevance to enabling the survey work.

2.2 THE SPECIFICATION

More detailed survey requirements will be described in a section called 'The Specification'. This will usually be separate from the preceding brief, but if circumstances permit, the two may be combined as part of the same document.

The specification should include the following:

- *Summary*: a résumé of the information provided by the brief.
- *Survey location:* an annotated map or plan indicating which areas are to be surveyed. These should be made available, wherever possible, in electronic format. If the contractor is required to obtain digital map data the costs incurred have to be considered. If different areas require differing survey techniques and methodologies, then these should be indicated separately. The map can also be used to provide other important information (e.g. access routes), where necessary.
- *The survey grid/co-ordinate system*: the following needs to be identified:
    - whether a temporary or permanent survey grid is to be established;
    - responsibility for doing so (usually the survey team);
    - accuracy of the location of grid intersections (usually ±0.1 m);
    - georeferencing either to an absolute position on the Earth's surface with accurate GPS/GNSS measurements, or relative to a base map by accurate measurements to permanent features that are visible on such maps, to allow the grid to be exactly re-located if necessary by a third party; and
    - the geographic coordinate system and projection to be used for reporting results (e.g. WGS84, UTM-WGS84 or a particular National Grid).
- *Survey type*: a statement of the geophysical technique to be used – examples might include:
    - magnetometer area survey;
    - earth resistance area survey;
    - EM soil conductivity area survey; and/or
    - GPR area survey.
- *Survey instrumentation*: it is not usually necessary to specify the make or model of equipment (however, these should of course be stated in any actual reports). However, all equipment used must be able to meet the required specifications. For example, while the sensitivity of fluxgate gradiometers may be sufficient for most sites, there may be cases where the higher sensitivity of alkali-vapour magnetometers is required (e.g. to detect weakly magnetic postholes) and where fluxgate gradiometers of a less-sensitive make are unsuitable. For GPR surveys, consideration should be given to the centre frequency of the antennas to be used and to the necessity for antenna shielding due to above-ground reflectors (including cables and operators).
- *Survey methodology*: a statement of methodology, including:
    - effective spatial resolution, and maybe traverse/line separation and inline sampling interval (see Part I, 3.4);
    - whether data should only be acquired by traversing lines in one direction (uni-directional);

- o whether particular care has to be taken to protect the topsoil from damage through heavy equipment or sensor arrays with inappropriate wheels; and
- o for earth resistance surveys, which electrode configuration should be used and with what electrode separation.
- *Data processing*: whether particular data processing steps are required. For example if topographic corrections are required for electrical resistivity imaging or GPR data, whether GPR velocity analysis, migration and three-dimensional rendering is desired. If such specific processing requirements are made the costs for these must be specified accordingly.
- *Interpretation*: the level of detail required during data interpretation. For example, in some instances it may be considered to be sufficient to highlight areas of the data that may have 'archaeological potential' (e.g. Level 1 investigation – Prospection), while in other situations the reconstructed shape of all buried archaeological features and differentiation from other anomalies is required (e.g. Level 3 investigation – Characterisation). As the effort in creating a certain level of interpretation is directly linked to the resources required (and thereby costs), this must be specified clearly at the outset.
- *The report*: a statement to the effect that all fieldwork, data processing and reporting should follow the recommendations set out in the relevant guidelines. State what format the softcopy should have (e.g. PDF/A, the ISO standardised archiving version of PDF), how many hard-copies of the report are required, and what arrangements are in place to deposit one of these with the regional or national heritage body.
- *Digital archiving*: a statement of what arrangements are in place to ensure that survey documentation and digital data are complied into an Archive according to current guidance (see Section 5, Data archiving) and who is to deposit these to which Archiving Body.
- *Access*: a statement of access arrangements, providing clarity on how access to the site is to be achieved, and any conditions on this, together with a statement of whose responsibility it is to obtain permission from the landowner and/or manager.
- *Legal and other provisions*: a statement of any legal or other limitations relevant to the survey (e.g. for protected monuments), and a clear statement of whose responsibility it is to acquire the relevant consents and licences in such cases, and when this is to be done.
- *Timetable*: a statement of time constraints (e.g. for access to site), and the date by when the report must be delivered.
- *Feedback*: a statement that the results of any subsequent trial trenching or other excavation will be made known to the geophysical survey contractor, and that any subsequent commentary by the contractor, will be included in the final project report, if appropriate.
- *Further information:* anything further of specific relevance to realising the objectives of the geophysical survey.

Note that any pilot survey should be the subject of separate and equivalently detailed documentation, although this may be undertaken in advance to inform the completion of a final specification.

3. THE SURVEY REPORT

One of the most important deliverables of a geophysical survey is the survey report. This should be a clear and succinct text supported by tables, figures, appendices and references as necessary. It ought to stand independent of supporting material and should combine the qualities of concise technical description linked to lucid and objective analysis and interpretation. It is desirable that in the most part it is intelligible to specialists and non-specialists alike. It should usually be accompanied by a statement of the authors' and contractors' professional qualifications.

The minimum requirements of such a report are summarised in the following list and described in more detail below.

- Title page:
    - title of report;
    - author(s);
    - contractor;
    - client;
    - report reference number; and
    - date.
- Summary of results.
- Introduction:
    - site location (including NGR);
    - site description/history; and
    - survey objectives.
- Methods (techniques and methodologies):
    - survey techniques used;
    - reasons for this choice;
    - date(s) of fieldwork;
    - grid location;
    - geophysical instruments used;
    - sampling intervals;
    - equipment configurations;
    - method of data capture;
    - method of data processing;
    - variables used for the above; and
    - method of data presentation.
- Results:
    - description; and
    - interpretation.
- Conclusions:
    - assessment of achievement (or not) of survey objectives;
    - results summarised;
    - implications;

- - geophysical research value; and
    - recommendations (if appropriate).
- Acknowledgements.
- Statement of indemnity.
- References: list of works referred to.
- Appendices:
    - technical details of techniques and methodology and
    - data (e.g. magnetic susceptibility tables; grid location measurements).
- Plans/plots:
    - a survey location plan demonstrating relationships to other mapped features and indicating the position of individual data grids (minimum scale 1:2500);
    - a greyscale plot of minimally enhanced survey data, for example using only grid balancing/edge matching (see Part IV, 2.2 ; preferred minimum scale 1:1000);
    - a greyscale plot of improved survey data (see Part IV, 2.1.1; minimum scale 1:1000);
    - a greyscale plot of processed survey data (see Part IV, 2.1.2; minimum scale 1:1000);
    - where appropriate (see Part IV, 2.2) a X-Y trace plot of improved magnetic data (for large sites a sample of the data might be plotted instead, to support the specific interpretation of anomalies identified from greyscale images); and
    - one or more interpretative plans/diagrams (minimum scale 1:1000).

3.1 SUMMARY

This should be a *précis* of the principal objectives of the survey and the extent to which they were achieved.

3.2 INTRODUCTION

This should provide the reasons for the survey, set against a brief description of the sites or areas concerned. It should include reference to solid and drift geology, soil type and local geomorphology. The archaeological background (if known) should be summarised and reference made to previous fieldwork and/or publications, as well as to other relevant information (e.g. from the aerial photographic record and/or any related field investigations).

Other introductory items include: dates of fieldwork, national grid references, any research objectives, legal status of sites, ground conditions, weather, hydraulic conditions (i.e. wetting or drying part of cycle, if known), site peculiarities, documentary history, and any other relevant information.

3.3 METHODS (TECHNIQUES AND METHODOLOGIES)

The methods statement should be a concise account of the survey techniques and methodologies used, referring to an appendix or to other appropriate sources for a more detailed description of standard techniques and methodologies.

This information should be followed by noting the methods of data processing and software used. Reference should be made to the plots presented with the report, how they were generated and explaining reasons for their choice, if necessary.

The information can either be provided as textual description or as tabular metadata. Where information is already available in tabular form it is not necessary to recreate it in prose.

3.4 RESULTS

This section is usually the most variable in content between one survey and another, and between different practitioners' descriptions and analyses of their respective results.

If more than one survey technique has been used it is usually best to describe each set of results and their interpretation under a separate subsection and then provide a joint interpretation based on all data. Similarly, where non-contiguous subdivisions of the survey area are involved, these might each be dealt with in turn.

Much will depend on the clarity and simplicity or – by contrast – the complexity, of the results as to how the report should proceed. Some authors may prefer to write a factual account of the survey results including a geophysical analysis of anomalies (e.g. approximate feature size and depth), followed by a section on their interpretation and discussion. An alternative is to set out a blend of objective descriptions and explanatory interpretations that draws upon supporting information from other sources (e.g. aerial photographs, augering, trial trenching). However, exhaustive narrative detail, anomaly by anomaly, is tedious and should be avoided (the use of tables is encouraged); instead, maximum use should be made of accompanying plots and interpretation diagrams. Where plots and diagrams are mostly self-explanatory, the associated text should be brief. It is important to adhere to the level of interpretation that was agreed in the project specification (e.g. highlighting areas of 'archaeological potential' *vs.* reconstructing the shape of buried archaeological features).

Most importantly, it must be expressed clearly how the interpretation was arrived at, and the division between objective reasoning and more subjective circumstantial inference has to be made clear. The interpretation of archaeological geophysical data inevitably includes surmise – and this should be encouraged – but the reader should be left in no doubt precisely where the areas of uncertainty lie. Confidence in the interpretation of geophysical survey data can only come from transparency of the reasoning that links data acquisition to processing and interpretation. This is the foundation of scientific endeavour.

3.5 CONCLUSIONS

The conclusions should address the survey results with reference to the original objectives. The overall archaeological significance of the survey findings can be summarised and conclusions drawn, where necessary, about the need for future survey or research. In developer-funded evaluations, unless it is explicitly requested in the specification, it is not appropriate for the contractor to launch into discursive assessments of archaeological importance or to make curatorial recommendations.

The names and affiliations of the authors of the report should be stated at its conclusion, as well as the date of its final draft (or this information could be supplied at the beginning of the report).

3.6 SITE LOCATION PLANS

In most cases these should be based on large-scale official national map data, displaying national grid coordinates as eastings and northings, and for which copyright permission must be obtained. Other base plans may be acceptable, so long as they allow the entire survey grid to be shown, and they include features that can be clearly and accurately re-located on the ground, or identified on the appropriate map with appropriate map coordinates.

The survey grid should be superimposed on such a base map, and the opportunity may be taken to number the data-grids for ease of reference from the text; or the survey areas may be shown by outline only. In either case it is necessary to ensure that the surveyed area is clearly indicated on the location plan. Areas of the grid covered by different techniques can be indicated by differential shading or colours. Grid location measurements can be included on the plan, so long as clarity is preserved, or can be tabulated in an appendix.

3.7 DATA PRESENTATION – PLOTS AND PLANS

Much as one may hope that readers will have assimilated all the written detail of the report it is probably true that the greatest attention is paid to the summary and conclusions, and especially to the accompanying plots and interpretation diagrams. These latter, then, should be of a very high standard and include common components (see Sections 3.8 to 3.11, Data plots). It is generally recommended to provide data plots as greyscale diagrams as these allow a consistent assessment of all data. The range of data values chosen for the greyscale is often adjusted to the plotted measurements, for example by calculating their standard deviation. However, in some instances it may be advantageous to plot results with a fixed data range so that different data-sets can be compared.

While colour diagrams may be useful, for instance for highlighting extreme data values, their print-reproduction or copying on black and white devices may make them incomprehensible when different colours may print as the same shade of grey. Colour diagrams may sometimes also be perceived as if all anomalies with the same colour may be 'the same', where in fact they just share the same range of geophysical measurement values.

The range of data values from magnetometer surveys can often be appreciated best if displayed as X-Y trace format (but not as 'wire-frame' diagrams) although this may not be practical for very large surveys, where the density of traces may create very confusing displays. Sometimes creating X-Y trace plots for small sections of a survey is the best approach.

Each plan and/or plot must have a scale-bar or annotated metric grid and an accurately oriented north arrow. The plot or report will specify 'which north' this arrow indicates (usually grid north, but possibly magnetic or geographic north).

Greyscale and X-Y trace plots must also have a range-bar, labelled with values and units, indicating the range of the variable depicted. Each plot should be annotated with the details of the type of enhancement used.

For 'vertical' data plots the scale of both axes has to be indicated. For GPR profiles the vertical scale is usually the two-way travel time. If an estimated depth scale is additionally included, there must be an explanation how it was derived (e.g. using fitting of hyperbolas to estimate ground velocities). For ERI profiles the vertical scale may be a pseudo-depth derived from the electrode separation (pseudosection). If an inverted resistivity section is shown the parameters of the inversion must be explained. If the ground level is significantly uneven (±0.5 m) along the survey traverse concerned, a topographically corrected section should be considered.

Legends must be provided that describe the symbols and conventions used.

As far as possible, separate plots should be at the same scale and orientation to enable direct comparison. A scale of 1:500 is often suitable, although scales as small as 1:1000 are acceptable for large surveys. Although it is strongly recommended that the location of anomalies (for example for subsequent excavations) are derived from the electronic versions of the data (e.g. in a GIS), it may under certain circumstances be necessary to derive such information from measurements on the data plots (e.g. when only a printed map is available in the field) and their scale should therefore be sufficient to allow for this.

Where the effective spatial resolution of measurement data is unsuitable (or inappropriate) for display as a raster image alternative visualisation may be required. This is often the case for magnetic susceptibility or phosphate surveys where point readings may be recorded with a fairly coarse spatial resolution so that they are best visualised as symbols of proportional size, or symbols with graded shading.

3.8 PLOTS OF MINIMALLY ENHANCED DATA

To assess the quality of data collection it is necessary to include a plot of minimally enhanced data. These are based on the raw data, compiled from the instrument readings over the survey areas (Schmidt 2013a). Hardly any processing should be applied to these raw data, but grid balancing/edge matching is usually acceptable so that a reasonable display range for all data can be found. There should be a clear description of any processing that has been applied.

3.9 PLOTS OF IMPROVED DATA

The minimally enhanced data may have 'defects' due to problems during data acquisition. These can either be issues related to the equipment (e.g. erroneous readings), errors of the operator, or the environmental conditions encountered during the survey. Data improvement is usually applied to the underlying units of data acquisition (e.g. data grids) before they are compiled into larger units (e.g. composites). Some of the defects can be corrected after data acquisition if they are sufficiently consistent, but usually some information is lost during this process. It is hence essential to acquire data of the highest quality so that as little as possible data improvement is necessary. For example, if the automatic data acquisition in a magnetometer survey is consistently started slightly before or after crossing the baseline of a data grid the results of a bi-directional ('zigzag') survey may looked staggered or sheared. The appearance of the data can be improved, but this leads to the loss of information at the start or end of each line and thereby introduces discontinuities between adjacent data grids. Other improvement steps may include drift correction, grid balancing/edge matching and Zero Mean/Median Traverse correction (although this may remove archaeologically relevant linear anomalies). Sometimes spike removal is also used already in the data improvement stage to facilitate grid balancing, but care has to be taken not to remove information that is required for subsequent interpretation. At least one plot of the improved data should be provided.

3.10 PLOTS OF PROCESSED DATA

For an untrained 'consumer' of the geophysical data the anomalies produced by buried archaeological features are often difficult to see in the improved data. It may therefore be necessary to apply filters to highlight and enhance these anomalies. Although many experimental attempts are usually made to enhance the geophysical data from a site, only the most representative of these need to be included in the report. It is important to remember that filters may change the shape and size of anomalies (especially high-pass filters) and data interpretation should therefore be performed only on the improved data.

Other geophysical processing may also be applied to the data if it allows to delineate better the underlying features (e.g. analytical signal for magnetometer data) or can help with estimating geophysical parameters (e.g. a feature's depth).

3.11 INTERPRETATIVE DIAGRAMS

In some cases the survey plots by themselves are of such clarity that further interpretative aid, beyond annotation and description in the report text, is unnecessary. However, it is usually essential to include a diagram, or diagrams, as a supplement to the interpretation provided in the text. It is recommended that such graphics are at the same scale as the survey plots, for ease of direct comparison, or can be provided at a smaller scale as an overview of the wider picture. In some instances, the plots themselves may be annotated, but this can be visually confusing and they should therefore always be accompanied by an un-annotated plot for comparison.

The creation of interpretative diagrams is not an 'exact science', and often involves the translation of a synthesis of various pieces of evidence into a single image. While such a diagram will convey much that is derived from a scientific analysis of the original data, it will also, to some extent, convey more subjective impressions. As stipulated above concerning data interpretation (3.4 Results), it is important that the distinction between geophysical facts and archaeological interpretation is clear. To achieve this it is acceptable to provide two diagrams: one that shows an explicit simplification of the geophysical data, and another one that shows a more subjective archaeological interpretation of the first. For the second type of diagram, particularly if it is the only interpretative diagram to be used, it is important that the graphical conventions convey the nuances of the interpretation, but are not misleading where there is ambiguity or uncertainty. For instance, bold lines and sharp edges should be avoided when attempting to delineate features that can only be interpreted tentatively. The use of too many conventions or colours can be confusing and should be avoided. A full, explanatory key of any conventions, symbols, and colours and shadings used is essential (see Part IV, 2.3).

4. DISSEMINATION

4.1 SOURCES OF INFORMATION

Information about geophysical surveys can often be obtained from regional or national heritage bodies, and in some countries even dedicated archiving facilities exist (for example the Archaeology Data Service (ADS) in the U.K.). Some country-specific information is summarised in a Wiki at www.archprospection.org/eacguidelines.

Additional information about specific surveys or projects can of course be found in the published literature (see, for example, references at the end). The leading journal for the publication of research and case studies is *Archaeological Prospection* (onlinelibrary.wiley.com/journal/10.1002/(ISSN)1099-0763).

The International Society for Archaeological Prospection (ISAP) was established in 2003 and is the main forum for communication within the discipline, including an email discussion group and a regular electronic newsletter. All practitioners are advised to join (www.archprospection.org).

4.2 DISSEMINATION REQUIREMENTS

Geophysical surveyors, and their clients, have a responsibility to ensure that a copy of the full survey report is deposited with the relevant regional or national heritage bodies.

These obligations will ensure that fundamental information on surveys is made available for consultation, and allow for the continued public accessibility of summary information through the sources and mechanisms listed above.

It is recognised that public dissemination may at times not be appropriate (e.g. in the case of sites vulnerable to looting, or where sensitive planning issues are at stake), but the principle remains that, excepting such circumstances, survey information should be made as widely accessible as possible. Client confidentiality can be respected for reports associated with a planning application, but these should also be submitted to the regional or national heritage bodies within a reasonable time.

It should be further incumbent on the geophysical surveying community not only to make available information on specific surveys, but more widely to continue to raise the profile of its research and results through education and outreach, using all available media.

5. DATA ARCHIVING

Most countries have national guidelines for the archiving of archaeological material from field survey and excavation, and some also have guidelines for the archiving of digital archaeological data. However, the archiving of geophysical data from archaeological projects has very specific requirements and these are comprehensively discussed in the document *Geophysical Data in Archaeology: a Guide to Good Practice (2nd edn)* (Schmidt 2013b). It is best practice to first compile the digital data from a geophysical survey project into an Archive (e.g. arranging the data files in a hierarchical folder structure) and second to deposit them with an Archiving Body (see Part I, 8). Although derived from guidelines for the ADS in the U.K. (Schmidt 2001) and Digital Antiquity in the U.S.A., the *Guide to Good Practice* has a wide international remit. All those involved in the acquisition and deposition of geophysical information will benefit from this guidance and are encouraged to implement it where practicable as current good practice.

As stated above, depositing a copy of the report from a geophysical survey with the relevant regional or national heritage bodies is the minimum requirement of dissemination. However, it has to be acknowledged that for many development projects the data from a geophysical survey may be the most important 'evidence' that remains of an archaeological site. Survey data should therefore be treated as an important primary source of archaeological information and archived as carefully as physical remains. It is crucial that a strategy is in place from the outset of a project that ensures adequate storage, security and long-term accessibility of the data. Some national regulations stipulate that data generated as part of the planning process must be archived appropriately.

The various archiving steps can be subdivided into two main stages: (a) the creation of the digital Archive from data and metadata[8] and (b) the deposition of the Archive with an Archiving Body for maintenance and preservation. These tasks require the allocation of adequate resources and they should be included into the project brief from the outset (rather than as after-thoughts) so that tenders from different bidders can be compared.

The components that form the Archive can be broken down as:

- Geophysics data:
    - working files;
    - preservation files; and
    - image files.
- Project material:
    - project notes and
    - project report.
- Project documentation:
    - geophysics metadata;
    - geophysics georeferencing;
    - project metadata; and
    - file descriptions.

The 'working files' are those that are used during the processing and may be in a proprietary format, but they will have the most detailed information and hence will be suited best for further analysis, if the original software is available. However, to allow for data analysis with other software and to make provisions for the migration of the Archive to other storage facilities in years to come, data must also be stored in a preservation format. The most basic format for gridded data is as a 'XYZ text file' whereby the X-Y coordinates of each grid node and its value ('Z') are saved as a triplet in a single line. For a wider discussion of preservation formats see Schmidt (2013b). The details that are otherwise stored in the proprietary working files should be provided explicitly as part of the 'geophysics metadata'. Subsets of the full metadata record are usually acceptable and Schmidt (2013b, Chapter 6) lists several such subsets. The metadata should be included in the survey report, preferably tabulated for ease of future reference.

Not all Archiving Bodies have the same functionality and several broad types can be distinguished.

1. In-House Archiving: a solution whereby the Archive is maintained by a contractor or academic department themselves.
2. File Repository: a commercial storage facility to which the Archive is submitted, providing guaranteed long-term preservation.
3. Managed Archiving: a file repository that also provides migration and indexing of the content of the Archive.

---

[8] Metadata can be thought of as a tabulation of information associated with the measurements.

4. Accessible Archiving: making a managed archive available to other users, usually over the Internet.

The costs charged for the deposition of the Archive will depend on the type of Archiving Body and it is therefore necessary to specify the type of Archiving Body required in the project brief.

6. LEGAL CONSIDERATIONS

The legal framework for the assessment and maintenance of cultural heritage varies considerably between different countries and states. The most comprehensive European agreement is the 1992 'European Convention on the Protection of the Archaeological Heritage (Revised)', the so-called Valetta Treaty (Council of Europe 1992) (bit.ly/136czi7). It mandates

> "…to ensure that archaeological excavations and prospecting are undertaken in a scientific manner and provided that: non-destructive methods of investigation are applied wherever possible…" (Council of Europe 1992)

Many national governments have put into place legislation that meets the obligations enacted in this international treaty. Some other international conventions are in place that, although not legally binding, are encouraging best practice in national legislation. An example is the 'Charter for the Protection and Management of the Archaeological Heritage (1990)', that was prepared by ICOMOS (1990) (bit.ly/16wk9Qi). It states, for example, that

> "…archaeological survey should be a basic obligation in the protection and management of the archaeological heritage. At the same time, inventories constitute primary resource databases for scientific study and research. The compilation of inventories should therefore be regarded as a continuous, dynamic process." (ICOMOS 1990)

and

> "It must be an overriding principle that the gathering of information about the archaeological heritage should not destroy any more archaeological evidence than is necessary for the protectional or scientific objectives of the investigation. Non-destructive techniques, aerial and ground survey, and sampling should therefore be encouraged wherever possible, in preference to total excavation." (ICOMOS 1990)

6.1 SITE ACCESS

Although geophysical survey is subject to the usual legal constraints concerning trespass there will be instances when a landowner's refusal to allow access can be overridden on the legal authority of a central or local government department. The contracted agents of the latter may thus be granted legal powers of entry.

Survey fieldworkers should, in their turn, ensure that every effort is made on site to be courteous and considerate in their dealings with landowners, local residents and other authorities or organisations. A high level of professionalism is expected at all times.

6.2 METAL DETECTORS

Governing the use of metal detectors, many countries have specific regulations in place that reflect the 1992 Valetta Treaty; it requires

> *"to subject to specific prior authorisation, whenever foreseen by the domestic law of the State, the use of metal detectors and any other detection equipment or process for archaeological investigation."* (Council of Europe 1992)

6.3 GEOPHYSICAL SURVEY

The above statement of the 1992 Valetta Treaty that specifically addresses metal detectors (see Section 6.2, Metal detectors) was by some countries also interpreted as referring to geophysical instruments as 'detection equipment' when the Valetta Treaty was enacted in national law, and thereby strict licensing issues for geophysical survey are enforced in these countries.

The operation of GPR equipment anywhere within Europe requires an appropriate licence and adherence to an agreed code of practice. All GPR equipment must be CE marked in order to demonstrate compliance with the European Radio and Telecommunications Terminal Equipment (R&TTE) directive 1999/5/EC (European Commission 1999) and the European directives on stray emissions (EN302 066 01 & 02). It is the duty of the manufacturer to ensure that equipment conforms to European legislation on stray emissions; self declaration by the users of the equipment is not possible! In addition, some European countries also require an operator license and all GPR users should conform to the European Code of Practice (European Telecommunications Standards Institute (ETSI) Guidance document ETSI EG 202 730 http://bit.ly/1kI85ll, which is based on EuroGPR's Code of Practice http://bit.ly/Rk0rFe). See Part IV 1.4.6 for more details.

PART III: CHOICE OF GEOPHYSICAL TECHNIQUE

1. INTRODUCTION

Geophysical survey is one of the main techniques of site evaluation and its potential contribution should always be considered where development is proposed.

As explained in Part I, the choice of geophysical survey techniques and methodologies depends on various factors and there are usually no simple rules for their suitability in a particular project. The purpose of the following section therefore is to highlight the considerations that should be taken into account when making a decision. It is always advisable to collect as much background information as possible and consult with experienced archaeological geophysicists on this matter. The following decision categories should be considered in turn. Clients must be assured that everything possible has been done to use appropriate techniques and methodologies in each project.

1.1 EXPECTED MATERIAL CONTRAST

The choice of geophysical techniques depends critically on the properties in which a geophysical contrast may be expected (e.g. magnetic, electrical resistivity). This in turn is dependent on the type of archaeological features anticipated, their material properties and the geological, pedological and environmental conditions of a site. Information about all these parameters is not always readily available and usually estimates based on comparable sites or pilot investigations have to be used.

The following example is an illustration of how material properties can influence the suitability of different survey techniques; each site will have its own characteristics, though. If the prevailing buried archaeological features are assumed to consist of architectural blocks made of local marble, and buried in soil derived from the same sources, the features as well as the soil would often have very low and similar magnetic susceptibility. The magnetic contrast between them would be small, or very similar to random variations of soil properties ('soil noise'). In these conditions magnetometer or magnetic susceptibility survey would probably not detect the features. By contrast, under reasonably moist conditions earth resistance or LFEM survey might show a contrast between the wetter soil and the highly resistive marble blocks. Best might be a GPR survey of the site which in these conditions would probably be successful under most environmental conditions due to the expected dielectric contrast between the solid blocks and the looser soil. However if ground salinity is present this would normally reduce the penetration depth of the GPR signal.

Based on regional experiences some authors have compiled tables to lists very generalised comments on the suitability of magnetometer survey for some major solid and drift geologies (e.g. English Heritage 2008, Table 4). The response of other geophysical techniques to differing geologies is even more difficult to categorise and is therefore seldom tabulated. The suitability of a particular technique should be assessed locally drawing on available expertise and knowledge.

1.2 SURVEY PURPOSE

As explained in Part I it is necessary to identify the level of investigation that a particular survey requires so that the most suitable survey methodology can be chosen.

- Level 1 – Prospection: to identify areas of archaeological potential and individual strong anomalies.
- Level 2 – Delineation: to delimit and map archaeological sites and features.
- Level 3 – Characterisation: to analyse in detail the shape of individual anomalies.

1.3 EXPECTED ARCHAEOLOGICAL FEATURES

Particularly for investigations of Levels 2 and 3 (Delineation and Characterisation, respectively) the expected arrangement, shape and size of archaeological features is important so that a suitable survey methodology can be designed with an 'effective spatial resolution' that allows resolving the necessary level of detail. The survey methodology may also depend on other characteristics of the site. For example if linear anomalies are expected (e.g. for a Roman villa) this requires the survey transects to be aligned at oblique angles.

1.4 LOGISTICAL CONSIDERATIONS

Although the above considerations should always take precedence, it has to be acknowledged that there are occasions when logistical (e.g. availability of equipment or expertise) and financial concerns may also have an important bearing on the selection of techniques and methodologies. As such extrinsic factors may severely impact the subsequent outcome of a project they should be clearly highlighted.

2. CHOICE OF GEOPHYSICAL SURVEY

Geophysical survey is of course one of many possible approaches to the evaluation of archaeological potential, and its contribution will be appropriately balanced with others so as to optimise the project outcome. A typical combination might include data derived from aerial photographs, map regression, geophysics, field walking and test-pitting. Ideally, datasets such as these will be analysed and interpreted within a GIS environment.

Within this broad concept of integration, geophysical survey itself offers a variety of approaches that can and should be used together to their mutual advantage. All projects need to give consideration to the full breadth of techniques that might be applicable to an evaluation, and to develop a specification that maximises their joint potential. For example, magnetometer survey may provide a distribution of pits, ditches and industrial features, but it will usually be necessary to combine this with more targeted earth resistance survey and/or GPR to identify building foundations. For the purposes of Prospection (Level 1), however, it may be sufficient for the chosen techniques to give just an indication of the archaeological potential; the use of more elaborate integrated survey strategies may be a feature of projects aimed at more detailed archaeological interpretations (Levels 2 and 3).

The sections below provide specific discussion of the survey options for a selection of common evaluation scenarios. More detail on aspects of technique and methodology can be found in Part IV. Furthermore, valuable complementary information is available in the following publications: Clark (1996); Gaffney and Gater (1993; 2003); Gaffney, Gater and Ovenden (2002); Linford (2006); Conyers (2012); Schmidt (2013a).

3. COSTS

Routine archaeological surveys are usually charged per hectare of area covered at standard sampling intervals. Such prices are usually inclusive of all aspects of the work and the supply of a report. However, in some cases – particularly when using less common techniques – quotations may not be all-inclusive and fieldwork may be charged per number of days on a site, with separate charges for data analysis and reporting. The costs of preparing the data Archive and depositing it with an Archiving Body are usually detailed separately. There may be a reduction in cost if multiple techniques are carried out on a shared grid. Prices can vary significantly between different companies and will of course vary according to constraints peculiar to each site. Clients are advised to obtain a range of quotations for detailed scrutiny, as the reason for a low price may be the omission of some deliverables. As with all other contracts, there is usually a correlation between the quality of the work undertaken (survey, processing, reporting, archiving) and the price quoted, and obtaining a sample report from a new contractor is therefore advisable.

On completion of the tendering process it is good procurement practice for the client to name the successful contractor, to declare the range of prices received and to provide a list of tender applicants. Any applicable legal requirements and public procedures regarding tendering and the award of contracts have to be followed.

4. URBAN AND BROWNFIELD SITES

The depth and complexity of most urban stratigraphy and of disused sites ('brownfield'), together with modern intrusions, metallic contamination, services and adjacent structures, pose considerable challenges for archaeological geophysical survey. An exception to this prognosis is when the survey is intended to detect the remains of industrial archaeology, which can often cause distinctive and very strong anomalies (e.g. boiler houses, firing pits). If techniques are carefully chosen to answer very specific questions, rather than undertaking a general Level 1 investigation (Prospection), useful answers may be derived. Close collaboration between the client and the geophysical team is essential.

Tightly constrained sites in heavily built-up areas do not usually offer suitable conditions for geophysical techniques, with the possible exception of GPR. This method is capable of detecting many types of archaeological feature (see Part IV, 1.4), and can also locate services and structural detail within building fabric. It is best applied when there is a measure of foreknowledge of what is sought, and preferably in conjunction with trial trenching or coring.

Magnetometer survey over tarmac is rarely successful. It may be possible over other types of paving but only in relatively unusual circumstances when no elements of the paved surface are strongly magnetic. Conventional earth resistance survey is not possible over tarmac or paved surfaces, but electrical sections can be collected using plate electrodes and conductive gel or bentonite clay (Athanasiou *et al.* 2007). Such surfaces are well suited to the use of GPR, and success has been reported with electrostatic techniques (Flageul *et al.* 2013).

On more open sites – rough ground, verges, gardens, allotments, playing fields, smaller parks, cemeteries, etc – the more traditional techniques can be applied, although experience shows that good results, while sometimes possible, are not often obtained. Surface obstructions or ground disturbance can prohibit sufficient survey coverage and compromise the survey response. Magnetometer, earth resistance and GPR methods can be invoked when encouraged by specific expectations (e.g. of kilns, voids or wall foundations). Decisions on survey technique and the interpretation of results will depend on a good knowledge of former land use. Trial trenching, coring and test-pitting may well be a preferable approach in many cases.

5. CEMETERIES

Survey within *present-day* cemeteries, for whatever purpose, is not very often successful. Earth resistance and GPR survey can be used where space permits, to identify or confirm the course of features the presence of which may already be suspected from other sources of information. In favourable conditions GPR survey may identify coffins or liquids released by recently deceased bodies, and in certain cases even edges of grave cuts. Note that in most countries permission needs to be obtained from church authorities prior to such a survey.

A more common task is the detection of *former* cemeteries or individual graves. None of the techniques described above can very easily detect individual inhumation graves or cremations owing to their relatively small size and lack of physical contrast between fill and subsoil. Stone-lined coffins or cists, on the other hand, may be detectable with earth resistance or GPR survey (Bevan 1991), using a narrow sampling interval (at least 0.5 m × 0.5 m for earth resistance survey; 0.05 m × 0.25 m for GPR). Ordinary archaeological graves in rural situations can sometimes be found with magnetometer survey, also with a narrow sampling interval. The magnetometer response to ferrous items, chariot fittings or individual weapons may give away the presence of graves, but it is frequently impossible to tell the difference between these few responses and the majority, which are caused by modern ferrous items (Cheetham 2005).

Individual cremation burials may have a slight magnetic contrast, which is usually positive due to the magnetic enhancement caused by microbial activity in the presence of the buried remains (Linford 2004). Some authors have also reported a negative contrast, which may be attributed to demagnetisation of soil during cremation (Fassbinder 2009). However, the magnetic contrast is often too weak to create an anomaly that can be definitively attributed to a burial. In such circumstances survey with very sensitive magnetometers (e.g. alkali-vapour) may provide the sensitivity that is needed for the detection.

Shallow ferrous and non-ferrous items such as coffin nails and grave goods are detectable electromagnetically with metal detectors, the supervised use of which can be valuable in the detailed study of sites or of individual graves (David 1994).

Graves, cremations or cemeteries can therefore only be detected in very favourable conditions, often only indirectly, and when there is already good reason to suspect such features to be present. Geophysical evaluation, particularly over poorly known ground, may therefore overlook this important category of feature.

6. ALLUVIUM

The detection of archaeological features at depths beyond 1 m, whether covered by alluvium, colluvium, blown sand, peat or other material, remains a problem. Archaeological features under river alluvium, in particular, have attracted much attention (Howard and Macklin 1999; Needham and Macklin 1992; Castaldini *et al.* 2007; Masini and Lasaponara 2007; Bruckner *et al.* 2006) and the problems encountered by geophysical techniques in these circumstances have been discussed by Clark (1992) and Weston (2001). The use of geophysical methods as part of a multidisciplinary approach to the geoarchaeological evaluation of deeply stratified sedimentary sequences has been addressed by a number of authors (see for example Bates and Bates 2000; Bates *et al.* 2007; Carey *et al.* 2006; Challis and Howard 2006; Powlesland *et al.* 2006; Kattenberg and Aalbersberg 2004; Verhegge *et al.* 2012; Bendjoudi *et al.* 2002).

There can be no preferred recommendation for survey technique and methodology, until the merits of each individual site or area have been assessed. A pilot survey, linked with coring or test pitting can be invaluable in the subsequent development of a preferred full evaluation. Depths of alluvial cover, magnetic susceptibility values for the major sediment units, and local geomorphology will all have a significant bearing. Aggregates companies may have commissioned borehole and other surveys that can be helpful. In some countries such information may be available from government agencies. Information on mechanical coring as an aid to archaeological projects has been published by Canti and Meddens (1998) and by English Heritage (2007).

Magnetometer survey is usually a well suited technique (see Part IV, 1.2). Depending upon the magnetic susceptibility contrast between the fills of smaller features, the alluvium and the subsoil, and the depth of burial, archaeological sites may be detectable up to a depth of about 1 m (Clark 1992). The deeper the archaeological features, however, the less likely to be resolved are small and poorly magnetised features. Magnetic anomalies broaden as features are more deeply buried by alluvium. While larger ditches, pits, hearths and kilns may well be detectable at depths beyond 1 m, the signal from smaller features will usually be too weak; many types of site – especially pre-Iron Age ones and those without significant magnetic enhancement (e.g. most 'ritual' and many ephemerally occupied sites) – can be missed altogether.

Magnetometer survey should preferably start with the shallower alluviated areas and their margins, and should, if possible, attempt to 'follow' detected features into areas of deeper alluvial cover, thereby enabling an estimate of 'fall-off' in local detectability. Close attention to available aerial photographic and microtopographical evidence is always essential.

Survey with alkali-vapour magnetometers, which have an increased sensitivity over fluxgate instruments (see Part IV, 1.2), makes it possible to detect weaker signals from more deeply buried features. It seems inescapable that the greater sensitivity of alkali-vapour instruments will offer an advantage over less sensitive instruments on sites where variations in topsoil magnetisation are minimal, as may be the case over some alluviated sites (Linford *et al.* 2007). The degree of that advantage, and its archaeological significance, will vary from site to site. For the time being, the use of alkali-vapour magnetometers should at least be a consideration in evaluations of alluviated areas where magnetic targets are concealed at depths beyond 1 m depth.

If magnetometer survey is ineffective it may be worth attempting earth resistance survey over suspected structural remains, but the reduced resolution at depth may be problematic (Clark 1992). Electrical resistivity imaging (ERI) can be of value in plotting larger features of the sub-alluvial surface (Bates and Bates 2000) and under suitable conditions GPR can be a more flexible and rapid method than ERI (see Part IV, 1.4).

Area survey of topsoil magnetic susceptibility can sometimes indicate general areas of anthropogenic magnetic enhancement derived from shallow archaeological horizons and may be useful for directing subsequent magnetometer survey. Magnetic susceptibility data may also help with mapping the alluvial edge if this is not otherwise evident from other data. Augering to obtain samples for magnetic susceptibility measurements from sub-surface horizons can be done to obtain control measurements, but is often too time-consuming for more extensive area surveys of magnetic susceptibility, phosphate or other soil property.

LFEM survey (conductivity and magnetic susceptibility) can be used to identify changes underneath alluvium. However, as with most geophysical techniques, the deeper the target the coarser is the resolution, and under thick layers of alluvium mostly geomorphological changes are detected. However, in some cases archaeological remains buried under alluvium were detected in LFEM data more clearly than in magnetometer and earth resistance surveys (De Smedt *et al.* 2013a). Similarly, the low frequency (<200 MHz) required for GPR to penetrate thick layers of alluvium leads to a considerably reduced spatial resolution so that broad features such as palaeo-channels and gross stratigraphy can be detected, but mapping archaeological features is usually difficult. While higher GPR frequencies would allow better spatial resolution the signal attenuation in conductive alluvial soils either prevents or seriously inhibits the detection of smaller archaeological features (see Part IV, 1.4).

In summary, extensive deep overburden, such as alluvium, presents considerable challenges for geophysical prospecting. These are accentuated at depths beyond 1 m. For large areas, a pilot survey can be conducted, testing the suitability of various techniques. Some survey techniques, such as GPR, can be used selectively, but at present none can be recommended as an adequate general technique in these conditions. While some alluvial archaeological sites may be detectable from the surface, it is likely that many others, perhaps even the majority, will remain elusive until revealed by more direct intervention (e.g. test trenching). However, the ability to detect larger geomorphological features, such as palaeo-channels, and the value these may have for indirectly predicting the presence of archaeologically significant deposits, should not be underestimated.

Whereas geophysics may be helpful in some circumstances, archaeological evaluation over deeper alluvium (>1 m) should rely on a combination of field techniques including intrusive measures.

7. WETLANDS

The problems of depth of burial, as described for alluviated sites, are accentuated by waterlogging. The only techniques that at present seem to offer any potential are LFEM and, to a lesser extent, GPR. LFEM measurements can be effective even on waterlogged sites (De Smedt *et al.* 2013a) where GPR signals may be unable to penetrate below the watertable. GPR surveys have been successful over peat of low mineral content, where at low frequencies (50-100 MHz) the peat/mineral interface of peat basins is detectable at depths of up to about 11 m (Theimer *et al.* 1994; Utsi 2001). Collecting peat samples for analysis from different depths in advance of the survey may allow selecting the most appropriate equipment and methodology. GPR reflections have also been recorded from substantial objects such as bog oaks (Glover 1987). Some case studies (e.g. Clarke *et al.* 1999) indicate that GPR is also capable of detecting potentially significant anomalies within peat, and there are reports that wooden trackways or other structures may be detectable (Jorgensen 1997; Utsi 2001). Although such accounts are promising, there is a need for further research and complementary information (e.g. excavation) before GPR can be recommended as a routine approach in these circumstances. In other types of wetland, in clay or saline situations, GPR and other techniques are ineffective at locating organic structures. Moderate success has been reported with induced polarisation (IP) imaging (Schleifer *et al.* 2002).

Geophysical techniques are overall less successful in wetland evaluation. Structural remains (such as pile dwellings, trackways, etc.) in organic sediments, in particular, are often not detectable with geophysics. Traditional dry-land geophysical techniques are best applied in areas of relative dryness and shallow overburden ('islands', or wetland margins) and features so detected may then have some indirect bearing on the likely location of significant sites elsewhere. Aerial photographs and remote sensing (Cox 1992; Donoghue and Shennan 1988), linked with augering and test trenching, can offer the best overall evaluation, geophysics being applied for the examination of specific shallow or marginal sites.

It should be noted that magnetic susceptibility readings on waterlogged material can be suppressed by chemical changes (Thompson and Oldfield 1986; Fassbinder *et al.* 1990). Magnetic susceptibility signals will persist in some lacustrine and intertidal deposits, however (Linford 2003; Kattenberg and Aalbersberg 2004).

8. ROAD AND PIPELINE CORRIDORS

The need to evaluate linear corridors traversing many kilometres of countryside in advance of the building of pipelines, new roads or the upgrading of existing routes, continues to create considerable demand for non-destructive evaluation (Campana and Dabas 2011). Geophysical survey thus has a crucial role in such linear developments and although the general rules of survey as outlined elsewhere in these guidelines apply the special problems of survey logistics, and the choice of an appropriate balance of survey methodology, suggest that a separate consideration is needed. Specifically, while linear corridors may be comparable in total area to the very large development areas described below in Section 10 (Very large areas), their narrow lateral extent makes them particularly amenable to detailed survey over the entire development area using modern survey methodologies. Hence the considerations in this section override those described below for very large development areas in general.

It is stressed that the following recommendations are general and do not attempt to set out a rigid procedural blueprint. As for any geophysical survey, individual site conditions will dictate a survey procedure that is expected to vary from one instance to another. Inevitably, different survey specialists will favour slightly different approaches. The following provides some considerations that should be common to all.

Linear developments are complicated by the large and extended area of land affected and by the variety of geological and soil conditions through which the route will inevitably pass. Geophysical survey may often play an important role in the evaluation of archaeological remains threatened by linear developments and should be conducted at an early stage in the planning process, when consideration of the results may mitigate the route of the development to take account of significant archaeological features.

While it is acknowledged that the destruction caused by the linear development is the main concern, consideration should also be given to the impact of the development on obtaining geophysical data in the future. In particular, ferrous pipelines will produce a large area of magnetic disturbance, up to 20-50 m to both sides of the pipe, which will compromise the subsequent acquisition of magnetic and electromagnetic data.

A balance will have to be met between the cost of obtaining adequate geophysical coverage, the impact of the proposed development and the anticipated benefits of the survey results.

The following specific points should be addressed:

1. The proposed geophysical methodology should be appropriate for the archaeological remains along the route of the linear development. The results of previous geophysical surveys conducted under similar conditions should be considered when recommending survey techniques and methodologies. Note that a single technique may not be suitable for the entire length of the proposed development.
2. Detailed area survey over a closely sampled grid is to be preferred over low sample density recorded methods (e.g. topsoil magnetic susceptibility). Where circumstances dictate that such methods should be used, single long traverses should be avoided.
3. The area covered by such detailed survey should be sufficient to encompass the entire easement of the development and any additional areas where damage to underlying archaeological deposits may occur (e.g. site traffic access routes). In addition, ferrous

pipelines will make future magnetic and electromagnetic survey impossible and a wide enough area should be investigated.
4. If possible, the survey transect should also be of sufficient width to characterise adequately the archaeological potential of significant geophysical responses, particularly linear anomalies, traversing the route. This may save the need for any subsequent requirement for additional survey to define further 'enigmatic anomalies'.
5. The recent introduction of multi-sensor geophysical instruments and platforms, combined with GPS/GNSS, has significantly increased the rate of field data acquisition. As a result, areas that in the past would have been considered so large that they could only be partially sampled, are often now amenable to rapid and cost-effective detailed survey in their entirety. In addition, not having to lay out grids allows efficient coverage even when an area is subdivided into several smaller fields.

Providing that no overriding geophysical contra-indications exist (e.g. unfavourable geology or soils, large numbers of modern ferrous interferences), then magnetometer survey may provide the most cost-effective method of investigation. For a Level 1 investigation (Prospection) a sample interval of 0.25 m × 1 m may be sufficient, but the interpretation of results will be more reliable if a denser line separation is chosen, which can be achieved fairly easily with multi-sensor instruments.

Although the potential benefits of additional geophysical techniques should always be considered, they will often only be affordable over large parts of a linear development, if there are particular reasons, similar to those discussed for very large areas of investigation (see Section 10, Very large areas).

The width of the corridor to be evaluated using geophysics will depend on the particular linear development in question. However, in the case of pipeline developments, given the typical easement width and the area excluded from subsequent survey by the presence of the ferrous pipe or embankments, a minimum linear transect width of 30 m would commonly be suitable. For road corridors the width is normally between 40 m and 100 m, and this should always be completely covered. Agreement should be reached with the client as to whether or not a broader coverage to the sides of the corridor may be allowable in order to place features within their broader context. Broader coverage may also be of benefit to the development, identifying potential alternative routes to be planned around areas where archaeological remains are identified. Clients or their agents should be encouraged strongly to allow for such contingencies, following appropriate consultation.

9. WIND FARMS

Wind farms require the construction of a group of turbines usually on a site in an elevated, exposed rural area. Owing to their nature, it is necessary for the turbines to be dispersed relatively widely across the landscape and each needs a firm foundation set into the ground. When considering geophysical evaluation of wind farm sites, it is preferable that the entire area over which the turbines are to be distributed is surveyed in detail. If areas of particular archaeological potential are identified, targeted follow-up survey with more intensive techniques such as earth resistance and GPR can then be used, as for other forms of development. With a full survey over the whole site it should be possible to select individual turbine positions so that the most archaeologically sensitive areas are avoided.

However, if turbine positions are constrained and the area of the entire site is so large that it is considered unreasonable to survey it all in detail, then consideration should be given not only to the physical foundation of each turbine but also to its magnetic footprint when installed. Wind turbines are typically tall steel structures that cause strong local magnetic fields, which will influence sensitive magnetometer measurements made in their vicinity. Once in place it will not be possible to detect archaeological remains using a magnetometer within a radius of about 50 m of the turbine. It is thus recommended that, at a minimum, detailed magnetometer surveys of 100 m by 100 m areas be carried out centred on each turbine position before their emplacement.

10. VERY LARGE AREAS

In some cases the total extent of a development may exceed the area that can be reasonably surveyed in its entirety. What is deemed to be reasonable will depend on several factors, not least of which will be the previously established archaeological sensitivity of the area in question and the available resources. The archaeological factors should always be the prime consideration and a full detailed survey will provide the best archaeological results. However, the investigation of such large areas is often undertaken to reduce the risk of finding archaeological remains later during construction work and such a risk is set against the fraction of the whole area that is chosen for survey.

It is important that the survey potential of any area is assessed in the light of existing archival knowledge (desktop assessment). If this does not provide sufficient information to determine the priorities for survey, and especially in the case of large areas, a pilot magnetometer survey can be carried out before any further commitment to major outlay of resources. Further preliminary field trials to assess responses to local conditions (pilot investigations) may also be warranted, and these could include other survey techniques, like magnetic susceptibility measurements, earth resistance surveys, as well as tests with LFEM or GPR.

In rural, semi-rural, and many other open areas, where magnetic interference is not too strong, it is advisable to undertake detailed magnetometer survey over the *entire* evaluation area, covering at least the ground that will be destroyed or damaged by the development. Increased archaeological sensitivity or other pressures may demand that in addition areas beyond the planned development are covered in detail.

The interpretation of the archaeological record will benefit from using additional techniques. However, earth resistance survey over large areas is currently only undertaken when it is clearly called for on the basis of independent evidence (see Part IV, 1.3), but with the ongoing development of wheeled and motorised systems such surveys are becoming feasible (Campana and Dabas 2011). In some cases they may even be a better means of archaeological evaluation. The same applies to GPR survey with wheeled multi-antenna systems, which nowadays also provide for rapid survey over large areas. The amount of data collected and hence the subsequent processing needed will be considerable and needs to be taken into account.

In exceptional circumstances, where full detailed survey of an area in its entirety is deemed impracticable, a compromise between this and less intensive sampling may be required, justified by the commissioning body. In these cases, again, magnetometer survey should usually be a priority. The following, or similar, approach may then be used.

1. Detailed geophysical survey of priority sites identified by a desktop study.
2. Geophysical coverage of a percentage of the investigated area. It is important to remember that the archaeological interpretation of a sampled and fragmented geophysical data-set can be very difficult. Sampling approaches should therefore preferably use large survey blocks, for example by leaving out areas around field boundaries. Long wide survey stripes are also a possibility, but chequerboard patterns of individual data grids should be avoided.
3. Where necessary for a confident archaeological interpretation blocks between the initially sampled areas may have to be filled in subsequently with additional geophysical survey.

If a geophysical sampling methodology has to be used, several issues should be considered.

1. If it is unreasonable to evaluate an entire development area using detailed area survey over a closely sampled grid, it is still desirable for at least 50% of the total area to be sampled with detailed measured survey.
2. If magnetic susceptibility measurements are used to fill in areas between sampled magnetometer survey single long traverses should be avoided and several parallel traverses separated by a distance similar to the measurement interval along the traverse should be recorded.
3. It is desirable that magnetic susceptibility measurements are followed up by complementary and more detailed survey in areas of enhancement. Some areas lacking enhancement should also be tested in this way to demonstrate that, for the area in question, variations in magnetic susceptibility are primarily caused by the presence or absence of archaeological remains and not by changes in other factors such as geology or recent land use. To assist interpretation, magnetic susceptibility values for different subsoil types should be obtained for comparison against topsoil values. If necessary this relationship can be examined further by comparison with fractional conversion

measurements. It should also be remembered that many archaeological sites do not show strong enough variations in topsoil magnetic susceptibility to be detectable (e.g. burial sites).
4. Single earth resistance or magnetometer traverses undertaken between the sampled areas are not useful.
5. Geophysical survey should, whenever possible, be complemented with aerial photographic investigation and analysis of topographic data (e.g. from LiDAR scans).

PART IV: INTRODUCTION TO ARCHAEOLOGICAL GEOPHYSICS

1. APPLICATION OF TECHNIQUES

1.1 THE SURVEY GRID

Geophysical fieldwork relies on the presence of an accurately plotted network of control points extending across the area to be worked on and this is usually referred to as the survey grid. An internally accurate and correctly georeferenced grid is crucial to all subsequent survey and to the whole project outcome. Close attention to this fundamental stage of fieldwork is therefore essential. Recent developments involving mobile sensor platforms incorporating real time global positioning system sensors (GPS/GNSS) mean that it is no longer always necessary to establish a conventional grid of fixed markers over the surface of the area to be surveyed (see Section 1.1.2, Interfacing with GPS/GNSS). When employing such technologies, survey teams should recognise that a grid of control points capable of defining accurately the boundaries of the area surveyed is still required even if not physically laid out with ground markers before or during the geophysical survey.

However the survey grid is located, during fieldwork a record should be made relative to it of surface conditions and sources of modern geophysical interference that might have a bearing on subsequent interpretation of field data.

1.1.1 Conventional survey grids
Establishing and marking out the survey grid are usually the responsibility of the project manager, although this should be discussed and clarified with the geophysical survey team involved. The grid can be laid out by any suitably qualified personnel with the agreement of (and, if necessary, following the instructions of) the geophysical surveyors. Considerations of geophysical methodology or ground response may well dictate a preferred grid alignment, particularly when the alignment of linear features is already known. In this regard, Gaffney and Gater (2003) provide a concise review of the issues common to most archaeological geophysical surveys.

Where deadlines are tight, a previously surveyed grid will allow the incoming geophysical survey team to concentrate their specialist time to greater effect. Where more time is available, they may otherwise wish to provide the survey grid themselves. Whoever lays out the grid, it is important that its internal accuracy and measurements to fixed topographic points are rigorously and independently checked. Geophysical survey teams are advised always to check the accuracy of previously surveyed grids and to take independent measurements for grid location. There can be no excuse for any subsequent mismatches between different parts of a geophysical survey, or other positional confusion. It is preferable and convenient, but not essential, for the geophysical survey grid to match exactly the national grid or a site grid devised for other purposes, such as field walking. The need to fit a survey into existing boundaries may dictate the use of a different grid, however. If more than one grid is used, accurate location of each will be critical for the subsequent integration of results.

A unit of either 20 m or 30 m for the side of each data grid is usual (although some survey methodologies may use a different optimal base survey unit), with grid intersections located on the ground using wooden or plastic pegs, or other temporary markers, which must be non-magnetic for magnetometer surveys. Because of the many hazards involved, not least of which concern the safety of people and animals, the choice of markers and their duration in the ground needs careful forethought as well as the agreement of the landowner and/or tenant (see also Part II, 6.1).

The grid should be laid out using currently accepted conventional methods (e.g. Bettess 1992; Bowden 1999; Clark 1996).

For long grid lines, in excess of 100 m, the use of a theodolite, EDM total station or GPS/GNSS is advisable. For smaller grids, the use of an optical square is acceptable (e.g. English Heritage 2002). English Heritage (2003) provides a useful summary of the different types of measurement accuracy associated with survey grids, defining relative, map and absolute accuracy. Using any of the aforementioned techniques it should be possible to locate the grid control points on the ground to a relative accuracy of ±0.1 m.

GPS/GNSS equipment is becoming increasingly available and English Heritage (2003) addresses the issues associated with its use for archaeological survey, classifying the various types of GPS/GNSS system according to the positional accuracy that can be achieved (navigation-grade, map-grade and survey-grade). Survey-grade GPS/GNSS, capable of absolute positional accuracy of ±0.1 m (either in real time or with post-processing), is the only grade suitable for locating survey grid control points. It should be noted that the positional accuracy of existing base maps may be lower, depending on how they were originally created (see English Heritage 2003). Bearing this in mind, it is advisable when using GPS/GNSS to locate the survey grid to measure the positions of some fixed local landmarks or boundaries recorded on the area base map and not just record the temporary survey grid points. Any discrepancies between GPS/GNSS positioning and local base mapping can then be compensated for and it is also possible to re-establish the grid independently relative to the measured landmarks.

1.1.2 Interfacing with GPS/GNSS
Recent developments in GPS/GNSS technology mean that it is now possible to interface geophysical survey instruments directly to continuously logging mobile (portable) GPS/GNSS sensors, enabling the position of each measurement to be located accurately as it is taken (*Figure 1*). A differential GPS/GNSS system may be employed to position

measurements rapidly relative to a field-based control station, which is subsequently georeferenced to provide absolute accuracy through post-survey processing. However, the most recent real-time GPS/GNSS systems can provide immediate survey-grade absolute accuracy by receiving broadcast signals from real-time correction signal transmitters calculated from a network of fixed control stations. With both types of GPS/GNSS systems it is possible to carry out an accurately positioned geophysical survey without first establishing a physical grid of ground markers. It is important for the users of such systems to be aware that the same considerations apply with respect to the georeferencing of the survey area as when GPS/GNSS is used to position a conventional survey grid. For instance, the speed of data acquisition might dictate that it is not possible to position every geophysical measurement directly to survey-grade GPS/GNSS accuracy. Because of such considerations the boundaries of the survey area have to be georeferenced accurately to the same standard as would be expected when a conventional survey grid is employed.

Figure 1: The GEEP towed mobile sensor platform with built-in GPS.
(photograph courtesy of Ian Hill, University of Leicester).

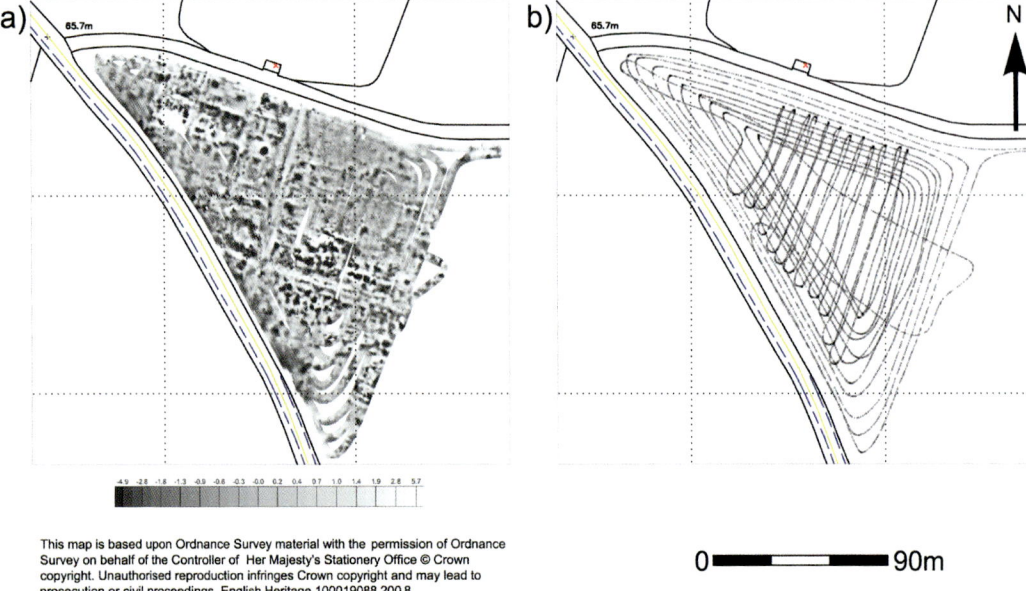

Figure 2: Field trial data collected at Wroxeter Roman city using the GEEP system. Data were collected with the system shown in Figure 1: (a) Greyscale plot of the caesium magnetometer results, which clearly show part of the Roman city plan; (b) Plot of the on-board GPS measurements showing the track of the system around the field; this was a rapid trial to test different survey methodologies and the southern corner of the survey, where gaps are visible between the magnetometer transects in (a), highlights the importance of ensuring even data coverage when not surveying on a regular grid (data courtesy of Ian Hill, University of Leicester).

Portable GPS/GNSS sensors mounted in a backpack or on a mobile sensor platform (see Section 1.7.9, Multi-channel instruments and sensor platforms) provide freedom from a grid of fixed control points. However, for geophysical survey two considerations should be borne in mind. Many geophysical instruments have a response that is conditioned by their direction of travel (e.g. magnetometers) and subtle archaeological anomalies may not be distinguishable in a survey where random measurement errors are introduced by frequent changes of direction. For this reason, a completely 'random walk' data-acquisition strategy is usually inappropriate for geophysical surveys. An even density of measurements should be achieved over the whole survey area, avoiding dense clusters of measurements in some parts and very wide gaps between measurements in others.

One way to avoid both problems is to emulate the parallel, evenly spaced, traverses employed in conventional surveys either by using a portable navigational control linked to the GPS/GNSS system or by establishing a series or regularly spaced aiming points at the edges of the survey area. When employing such methods to ensure even coverage, care should be taken to avoid veering too far off-line when surveying each traverse as this could result in overly wide gaps between adjacent traverses resulting in gaps in the geophysical coverage (*Figure 2a*). To demonstrate that an even coverage has been achieved when not using a conventional grid, the point cloud of measurement positions should be plotted on the base map in the survey report (e.g. *Figure 2b*).

1.2 MAGNETOMETER SURVEY

1.2.1 Choosing magnetometer survey

Magnetometer survey offers the most rapid ground coverage of the various survey techniques and responds to a wide variety of features derived from past human activity. It is thus usually the first technique considered for detailed survey of an area and other, slower, techniques should usually follow afterwards, targeting smaller areas of interest identified by the larger magnetometer survey. It can identify thermoremanently magnetised features such as kilns and furnaces as well as in-filled ditches and pits and areas of industrial activity (both recent and ancient). Magnetometers do not usually detect wall footings directly unless composed of materials that contrast magnetically with the surrounding soil (e.g. bricks carrying a thermoremanent magnetisation). In these cases it should be complemented by earth resistance survey.

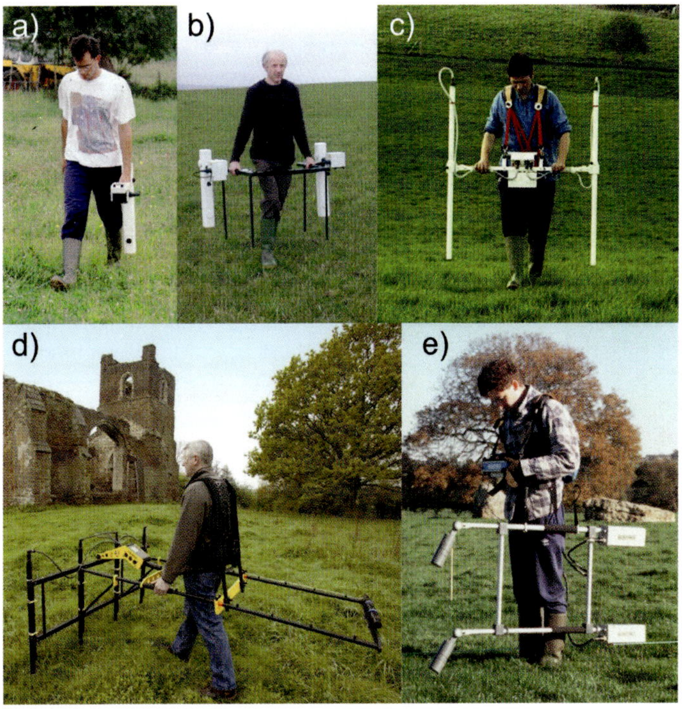

Figure 3: Handheld magnetometer systems.
(a) Geoscan FM36;
(b) Geoscan FM256 in dual sensor configuration (photograph courtesy of Roger Walker, Geoscan Research);
(c) Bartington GRAD601 dual channel fluxgate system;
(d) Foerster FEREX 4-channel fluxgate system (photograph courtesy of Norman Bell, Allied Associates Geophysical Ltd);
(e) Scintrex SM4G Caesium magnetometer.

1.2.2 Instrumentation

The main instrument for routine magnetometer survey in many archaeological projects is the fluxgate gradiometer. This instrument combines sensitivity of the order of 0.1 nT or better with lightweight design and rapid measurement rates, and several commercial systems are now available (*Figure 3a-d*). Alkali-vapour magnetometers (*Figure 3e*), also referred to as optically-pumped or caesium magnetometers (although the other alkali metals – potassium and rubidium – can also be used) offer sensitivities of the order of 0.05 nT (or below 0.01 nT, depending on the sensors used) and can make measurements at similar rates to fluxgate systems (typically 10 Hz).

The main practical difference between the two types of instrument is their sensitivity (Becker 1995), but to take full advantage of the higher sensitivity of alkali-vapour systems it is usually necessary to mount them on some form of mobile platform or cart (*Figure 4a-b*) – thus reducing sources of random measurement errors. The increased sensitivity is of particular importance on sites where the soil exhibits very little magnetic variation ('soil noise'), so that even very weak magnetic anomalies (e.g. from small post holes) can be detected in the data. This is particularly the case in the loess plateaus of Europe, where even very weak magnetic signals (e.g. from magnetotactic bacteria in

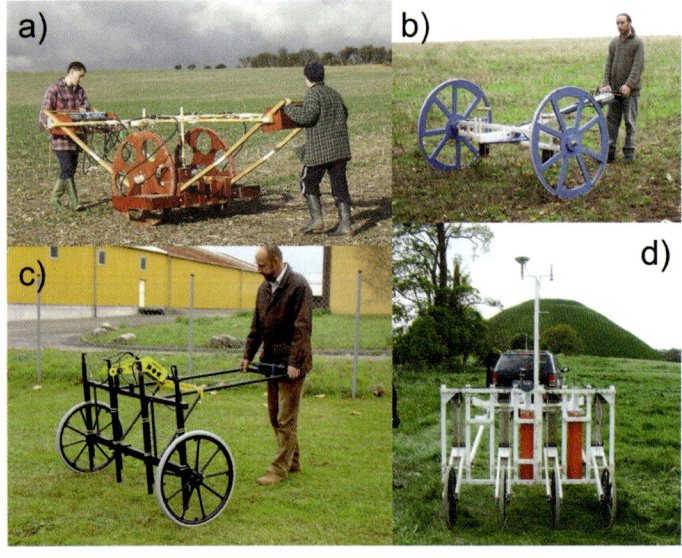

Figure 4: Cart mounted magnetometer systems. (a) Four Scintrex SM4 caesium sensors mounted at 0.5 m intervals; (b) two Geometrics G858 sensors mounted at a 1.0 m interval (photograph courtesy of ArchaeoPhysica Ltd); (c) Foerster Ferex 4.032 4-channel fluxgate system with sensors mounted at 0.5 m intervals (photograph courtesy of Institut Dr Foerster); (d) two sets of SQUID gradiometers mounted at 0.5 m interval.

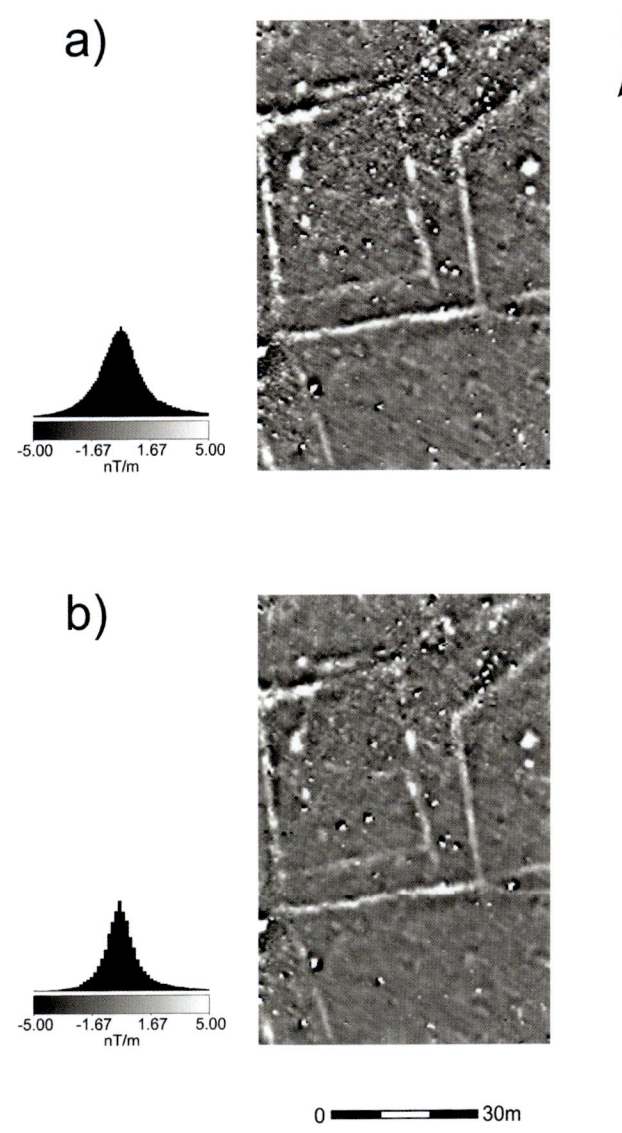

Figure 5: Greyscale plots of caesium (a) and fluxgate (b) gradiometer data. All data were acquired over the same Roman enclosures at the same sample intervals (0.5 m traverse separation and 0.125 m measurement intervals along traverses). Instrumentation: (a) Scintrex SM4G and (b) Bartington Grad601 sensors in 1 m vertical gradiometer configuration.

postholes (Fassbinder and Irlinger 1994)) can be detected against the 'magnetically quiet' background of the loess soil. In other regions (e.g. most of the U.K.), the higher sensitivity only seldom leads to the detection of additional weak archaeological anomalies; even a sensitivity of 0.1-0.3 nT has been found to be sufficient there (*Figure 5*). A high spatial sampling density, however, always leads to improved interpretability of results.

Alkali-vapour magnetometers measure the magnitude of the magnetic field and are hence far less sensitive to the sensor orientation ('heading error') than fluxgate sensors, which only measure a single magnetic field component (usually the vertical one). These sensors therefore have to be operated as gradiometers consisting of two sensors positioned one above the other (separated typically by a baseline distance of 0.5 m or 1 m). The arrangement allows removing the part of the magnetic field that is common to both sensors (mainly the Earth's field and its temporal variations) and reduces the directional errors. Although alkali-vapour magnetometers are also sometimes used in gradiometer configuration to eliminate the diurnal variation of the Earth's field, they can also be used with a fixed reference base station (variometer) or even as single sensors. In that case only short survey lines are usually recorded that can later be levelled to remove background variations. Such a configuration has advantages in uneven terrain, since it is more tolerant towards a tilting of the sensors.

Other types of magnetometer are also available (e.g. proton free precession, Overhauser, SQUID), but their use for routine survey would require special justification. Whatever type of magnetometer is employed, the operator should be fully familiar not only with the manuals supplied with it (and any updates provided by the manufacturer), but also with the physical principles of the instrument, and should rigorously apply the recommendations for equipment maintenance and survey procedure.

A number of manufacturers have adapted their systems to allow multiple sensors to be mounted horizontally in parallel. This enables two or more traverses of data to be collected simultaneously, increasing the speed at which surveys may be carried out. While this is a relatively recent innovation in the case of most fluxgate systems (*Figure 3b-d*), multiple alkali-vapour systems, often deployed on custom-built carts, have been in existence for some time (*Figure 4a-b*). Cart-mounted arrangements are also now being developed for some fluxgate systems (*Figure 4c*). For any type of magnetometer, these offer the benefits of reduced random measurement noise and rapid area coverage (a larger number of sensors may be mounted in parallel, typically enabling four to six multiple traverses to be measured simultaneously, potentially with an integral GPS/GNSS for positioning). Set against this, carts can be more restricted in the types of terrain in which they can operate as compared to light-weight, hand-held instruments, especially where the survey area is small and constrained, so a range of field conditions can mitigate in favour of the latter (Gaffney and Gater 2003).

1.2.3 Methodology
Before beginning a survey the magnetometer must be correctly prepared for use. Most magnetometers require some warm-up period before they settle into stable operation. This is typically of the order of fifteen minutes for alkali-vapour instruments but fluxgate gradiometers, being more sensitive to differences in temperature, typically require about twenty minutes to adapt fully to site conditions. Most fluxgate gradiometers must then be 'balanced' (aligning the two fluxgate sensors along the vertical axis) and 'zeroed' (calibration of the measurement scale for the local conditions). This procedure should usually be done over an area of uniform magnetic field, preferably using the same location throughout the survey. Particular care must be taken in the selection of this location when

calibrating dual- or multi-sensor instruments as a proportionally larger area free of local magnetic field perturbations is required.

The operator must remove all sources of magnetic interference from his or her clothing and body (note: coins cannot now be assumed to be non-magnetic). Particular care must be taken to ensure that footwear is not magnetic and that even small extraneous ferrous items (staples, studs, tags, springs in zippers, fasteners or underwire in bras) are not present in clothing. Note also that magnetic material (including excessive amounts of soil) can become attached to footwear (and sometimes even to the instrument itself) during the survey and can adversely influence the magnetometer signal where the soil is strongly magnetic. Clients should appreciate that there are some circumstances (e.g. soil on footwear) that cannot be easily avoided and may therefore result in a slight deterioration in data quality. If that is suspected, it should be highlighted in the report.

Field conditions may dictate the type and configuration of magnetometers that are most practical to employ. For instance, a cart-based system may be of limited use in a confined area. Gradiometers discriminate more strongly than total-field systems that consist of individual sensors, in favour of anomalies in close proximity to the sensors (Breiner 1999). This property can limit the maximum depth at which features may be detected and single-sensor total-field systems may be more suited when remains are expected to be buried deeply (e.g. alluviated environments). However, gradiometers especially with shorter baselines, can survey in closer proximity to modern ferrous objects such as wire fences or pylons. Indeed, this configuration is often the only way to carry out a magnetometer survey near a busy road as it reduces the effect of transient magnetic anomalies caused by passing vehicles, which cannot be readily filtered out by post-processing. Most archaeological features will produce only weak magnetic anomalies, so magnetometers with several range settings should be set at their most sensitive and certainly ought to be configured to measure differences of the order of 0.1–0.3 nT. However, in some instances (e.g. when surveying over industrial archaeological remains or substantial kilns or furnaces) reduced sensitivity may be necessary to avoid saturating the sensors when mapping very high magnitude anomalies.

Given the considerable speed (and thus cost-effectiveness) of modern magnetometers, the preference should be for a detailed magnetometer survey of the entire area subject to evaluation. The area to be surveyed is typically divided into a series of regular square or rectangular data grids (see Section 1.1.1, Conventional survey grids) and each is then methodically surveyed by conducting a series of equally spaced parallel traverses across it with the magnetometer. Measurements are recorded at regular, closely spaced, intervals along each traverse. This is usually achieved by setting the instrument to take readings at fixed time intervals and using an audible time signal to ensure an even pace, or by recording fiducial markers at regular distances so that variations in pace can be subsequently corrected for. However, as noted in Section 1.1.2 (Interfacing with GPS/GNSS) some recent magnetometer systems can integrate directly with a GPS/GNSS system to log the position of each measurement and obviate the need for a pre-established survey grid.

For detailed area survey it is strongly recommended that the maximum separation between measurements along a traverse should be no more than 0.25 m. Clark (1996) considered the sample resolution necessary to discriminate between near surface ferrous objects and more deeply buried archaeological features and concluded that a sample separation of 0.25 m enables full characterisation of anomalies with minimal distortion to their shape. Schmidt and Marshall (1997) examined the same problem from the perspective of the sampling theorem. They concluded that the sampling interval should not exceed the burial depth of the features being searched for. As the shallowest features may be in the topsoil, typically some 0.2–0.3 m beneath the magnetometer sensor, a sample interval of 0.25m is again recommended.

Modern magnetometers can sample rapidly (approximately 10 times per second), have data loggers with large internal memory capacities, and can quickly transfer stored data to a computer. Hence, sample density along traverses has relatively little impact on the time taken to survey an area. However, the same is not true of the separation between traverses where the time taken is nearly inversely proportional to the traverse separation (closer traverse separation increases the number of times the magnetometer is traversed across the area to achieve the necessary coverage). As explained in Part I, 3.4 the effective spatial resolution of a survey depends mainly on the traverse separation and only for Level 1 investigations (Prospection) may a 1 m separation be sufficient. If individual archaeological features are to be investigated (i.e. for most Level 2 and all Level 3 investigations, Delineation and Characterisation, respectively) a closer traverse interval is required (e.g. 0.25 m) and 0.5 m is a good compromise for most investigations.

Figure 6 illustrates the resolution of magnetometer surveys at a variety of sampling densities over two circular arrangements of postholes. The most dramatic increase in the ability to resolve the anomalies caused by these small features is achieved when the traverse separation is reduced to 0.5 m. The commensurate increase in survey time required to cover areas at this greater traverse density can be reduced by the use of multi-sensor systems (*Figure 4*). Multiple alkali-vapour sensors can be mounted at separations of 0.5 m and a similar effect can also be achieved with sensors fixed 1 m apart (e.g. with typical dual sensor fluxgate systems) by the use of interleaved traverses (Gaffney and Gater 2003).

Boundaries such as hedges and fences will often constrain the orientation of the survey grid. However, where possible, it is preferable for traverses to be walked at right angles to the direction of recent ploughing to minimise any adverse effects of the latter on subsequent plots. Where the alignment of anticipated linear archaeological features can be predicted in advance (perhaps from air photographic or earthwork evidence), it is again preferable to avoid orienting traverses in this direction. Linear anomalies parallel to magnetometer traverses can be inadvertently removed by processing to counter the directional sensitivity of the instrument. The most characteristic variation of an induced magnetic anomaly is along the magnetic north-south direction (being symmetric east-west), which simultaneously also produces the largest peak-to-trough variation (Breiner 1999). Therefore, when employing a sampling interval along the instrument traverses narrower than the separation between them and if there are no other constraints on traverse orientation, a north–south orientation may be beneficial. However, the design of the magnetometer used may also have a bearing on the best orientation of a survey grid and should therefore also be considered. Fluxgate gradiometers that need to be adjusted prior to survey require alignment with the magnetic cardinal directions during this process. It is therefore only in these directions that they are well balanced and survey traverses in any other direction may produce stripy data. Similarly, alkali-vapour magnetometers that are arranged such that electronics, cables and sensors are aligned to the survey direction are best operated along east-west traverses since disturbances from electronic and mechanic components are minimised in this direction.

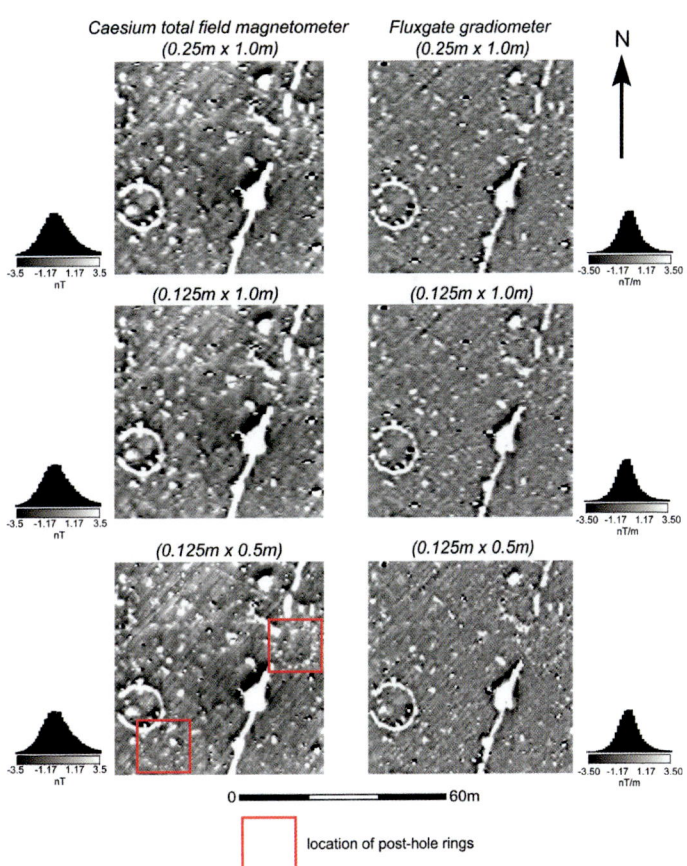

Figure 6: Caesium magnetometer and fluxgate gradiometer data collected at varying sample intervals. The data illustrate the advantage of increased traverse density for detecting discrete anomalies.

Fluxgate magnetometers can exhibit strong sensitivity to motion-induced errors when oriented in a direction to the Earth's magnetic field that is different from the four cardinal directions in which the alignments were adjusted prior to survey; the worst direction being specific to each instrument. Taking the traverse direction into account, care should be taken to avoid surveying with the magnetometer while oriented in this adverse direction, changing the way the instrument is carried if necessary. A similar consideration applies with respect to alkali-vapour sensors, which are insensitive to magnetic fields in directions aligned too closely to a particular direction dictated by the sensor's geometry known as the tumble angle. Again, care should be taken to ensure sensors are aligned appropriately for the local magnetic field direction.

Instrument traverses may be recorded in either 'zigzag' (bi-directional) or 'parallel' (uni-directional) manner (Gaffney and Gater 2003, Fig. 10), with data logger settings and subsequent data handling varying accordingly. While zigzag traverses enable the most rapid ground coverage, there can be a tendency for the response of alternate traverses to be offset with respect to one another, mostly due to slight timing differences between start/stop of the recording and the crossing of the magnetometer over the baseline of a survey grid. This can occur when the magnetometer is not held in the correct relative position or because of an incorrect walking pace relative to a trigger rate. The effect is often most pronounced when traverses run up and down slopes and results in linear anomalies at right angles to the traverse direction being 'staggered' and producing a herring-bone pattern. The worst effects of this problem can be eliminated by post-processing, but are often difficult to remove entirely. Hence for portions of a survey over particularly difficult terrain, parallel traverses should be considered and in all cases care should be taken to eliminate the effect as far as possible by correct data collection procedures.

While most magnetometers now boast non-volatile storage capacities capable of storing more than a day's worth of surveying, it is advisable to transfer data more frequently to a portable computer with subsequent backups to avoid excessive data loss in the event of an instrument malfunction. Frequent checks of the data being collected are also advised to ensure that adverse site conditions or faulty instrumentation are not compromising quality. Surveyors need to be alerted to factors such as the incorrect balancing of the instrument and the possible presence of magnetic contamination on the operator, as both can significantly distort data. If the magnetometer is responding poorly to local conditions then adjustments to the survey procedure should be made to compensate for these. To guard against unexpected failure of the portable computer, data should also be backed up to a suitable secondary storage medium at the end of each day's surveying.

1.2.4 Units of magnetic measurement

Magnetometers measure changes in the Earth's magnetic field and the SI unit of magnetic flux density is the Tesla (T) (Moskowitz 1995; Payne 1981; Taylor 1995). However, this unit is inconveniently large with respect to the weak magnetic anomalies caused by archaeological anomalies, so magnetometer measurements are normally quoted in nano-Tesla (nT) where $1\ nT = 10^{-9}$ T. Gradiometers measure the difference between two magnetic measurements separated by a fixed distance and this difference, the gradiometer response, is therefore also expressed in nT. If the source of the magnetic anomaly were very deep compared to the sensor separation (the gradiometer baseline) the ratio of 'gradiometer response/baseline separation' would be similar to the gradient of the magnetic flux density, which is expressed in nT/m. However, for most archaeological investigations this is not the case and only the very short baseline of SQUID gradiometers (e.g. 5 mm) warrants the expression of results as a magnetic gradient. However, in any case the gradiometer baseline used has to be noted and stated in the report so that results from different instruments can be compared more easily.

1.2.5 SQUID magnetometers
While relatively common within laboratory-based instruments that measure extremely weak magnetic fields, superconducting quantum interference devices (SQUIDs) are challenging to deploy in the field because they require very low operating temperatures. Zakosarenko *et al.* (2001) demonstrated that SQUID-based systems can also be used for measuring magnetic field gradients and have developed a field instrument specifically for archaeological prospecting (Chwala *et al.* 2001; Chwala *et al.* 2003; Schultze *et al.* 2008; Schultze *et al.* 2007).

This system is based on a cart-mounted liquid helium cryostat that is able to maintain a Niobium SQUID at a working temperature of 4.2 K configured as a special planar intrinsic gradiometer where the two effective sensors are extremely close together (*Figure 4d*). The magnetic field resolution of the SQUID is approximately 0.00002 nT, about 200 times greater than currently available alkali-vapour magnetometers, and possibly exceeds the sensitivity required to map even the weakest archaeological anomalies encountered in the field. However, this sensitivity is essential for operating as a gradiometer with such closely separated sensors, where the measured gradient will be extremely small, but will also be less affected by local distortions in the Earth's magnetic field. This, for example, allows the SQUID sensors to be transported in relatively close proximity to a towing vehicle with any residual field removed through post-acquisition processing. SQUID sensors allow much higher samplings rates than conventional magnetometers (approximately 1000 Hz), making them ideal for rapid data acquisition over large areas when operated as a vehicle-towed array. Although the short gradiometer baseline reduces the signal from deeply buried features, their high sensitivity nevertheless allows for the detection of some deep structures.

1.3 EARTH RESISTANCE SURVEY

While research continues to produce many refinements to the electrical prospecting technique, for most field evaluations that require an electrical technique, standard earth resistance survey is needed. Details of theory and field procedures have been extensively discussed in the literature (e.g. Clark 1996; Gaffney and Gater 2003; Schmidt 2013a) and instruction manuals (e.g. Walker 1991). Hence, the following guidelines do not aim to provide detailed theoretical or methodological information but simply set out basic parameters of good practice.

1.3.1 Choosing earth resistance survey

The rate of coverage using earth resistance survey is limited by the need to make direct electrical contact with the ground by the insertion of electrodes. A number of developments, such as mounting electrodes on a fixed frame as well as automated measurement and data recording have greatly increased the speed at which this can be done. Some cart systems have also been developed and motorised trapezoidal arrays are also in use (Campana and Dabas 2011). The rate of ground coverage of manual surveys typically remains about half that possible using a magnetometer, so survey costs per unit area are generally higher. It is thus particularly important that earth resistance survey is used economically and in circumstances suited to its particular strengths.

Earth resistance survey can often identify ditches and pits because they retain more (or sometimes less) moisture than the surrounding soil (Dabas 2006). However, in many instances the chances of detecting these with a magnetometer are higher and this more rapid technique is often preferred. Exceptions might be considered in areas of extreme magnetic interference or where soil and geological conditions are not conducive to the development of anthropogenic magnetic anomalies. Conversely, earth resistance survey should be favoured where building foundations and other masonry features are suspected, for instance over Roman villas, ecclesiastical and other medieval buildings, defensive works, etc. When applying earth resistance survey there should already be a strong presumption that such features exist within the survey area. In this sense, earth resistance is seldom a primary prospecting technique (Level 1) and its application in many evaluations will be secondary (Levels 2 and 3, Delineation and Characterisation). However, with advancements in motorisation of earth resistance arrays even large-scale investigations are becoming feasible and where the electrical contrast of archaeological features is much stronger than the magnetic one, they may be a better Level 1 technique.

Magnetometer and earth resistance survey complement each other (*Figure 7*) and, for large evaluations, it is often best to assess the area magnetically first, followed by selected earth resistance survey of areas identified as likely to contain building remains. Choice of survey method is rarely so simplistic, however, and will depend upon a balanced expert consideration of each separate situation. Those who commission geophysical evaluation should ensure that the particular works proposed are adequately justified prior to the settlement of the contract; this is best done in discussion with experienced archaeological geophysicists, and possibly after a pilot survey. It is especially important to be certain whether or not earth resistance survey is appropriate.

1.3.2 Instrumentation

While some of the earlier resistance meters such as the Bradphys and Martin-Clark systems are still in use, they do not provide the pace of operation or data handling facilities of more modern instruments. The most commonly employed resistance meters for contemporary area surveys make measurements automatically when electrical contact is made with the ground and can record readings to on-board electronic memory. Some of those particularly developed for archaeological applications (*Figure 8*) are particularly

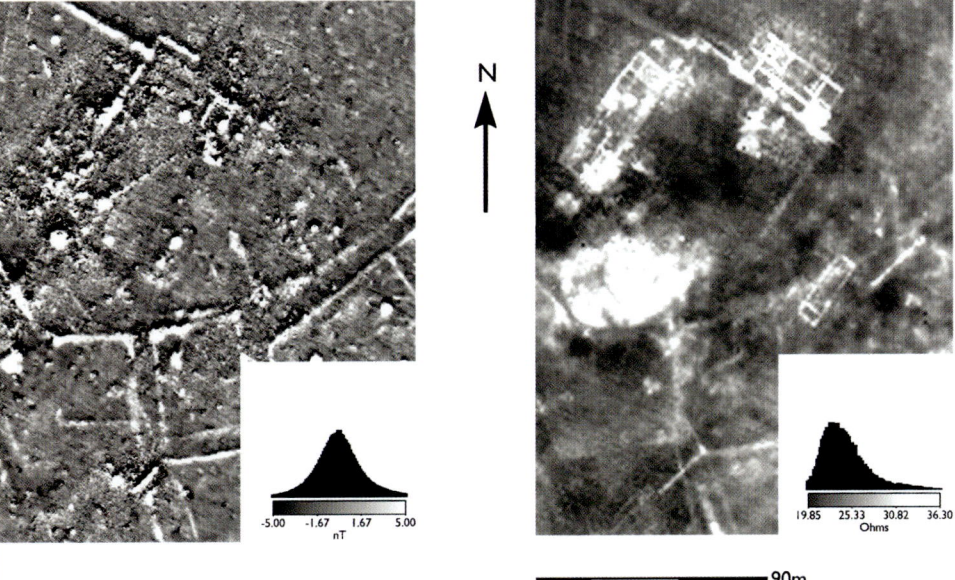

Figure 7: Caesium magnetometer (a) and earth resistance (b) survey of the same area.
The data are from a Roman site in Hampshire. Both techniques detect ditches, but the earth resistance survey reveals wall footings in clear plan where the magnetometer survey shows just magnetic 'noise' from ceramic debris.

versatile, with optional modular extensions for up to six multiplexed electrodes. Under favourable conditions several measurements at different electrode separations may be made each time the frame contacts the ground; one application of this facility is to speed up data collection by recording two parallel traverses of data simultaneously. Recent innovations have allowed earth resistance meters to be used with cart-based platforms on which spiked wheels replace the traditional electrodes. These platforms offer faster rates of ground coverage and it is often possible to mount other instruments, such as GPS/GNSS receivers or magnetometers, for simultaneous coverage (Dabas 2009).

1.3.3 Methodology
The type and standards of grid layout are the same as for magnetometer survey. For area evaluation surveys the twin-probe configuration (Clark 1996) will normally be employed. Using this configuration, many buried features are detected as single-peaked anomalies, and although the shape of the anomaly depends on the orientation of the electrode array (Schmidt 2013a) this dependency is for practical purposes relatively weak (Aspinall and Lynam 1970). Cart-based systems may, alternatively, use the square array, which has similar response characteristics but avoids the need for fixed remote electrodes. Three

different measurement configurations can be used with a square array (usually termed *alpha*, *beta* and *gamma*) and each is preferentially sensitive to anomalies running in a particular direction (Aspinall and Saunders 2005). Hence, it is recommended that both *alpha* and *beta* measurements are simultaneously made over a survey area when using the square array so as to detect the majority of relevant anomalies.

Clark (1996) considers optimum electrode separation for the detection of features buried at different depths. However, it is rare that the precise burial depth of archaeological features is known in advance and, for the twin-probe array, a mobile electrode separation of 0.5 m is now common and usually detects features up to 1 m beneath the surface. Where deeper overburdens are expected, a separation of 1 m is commonly employed. Electrode separations much greater than 1 m tend to result in multiple-peaked anomalies even over simple features and often result in considerable loss of definition. Modern multiplexers and modular frames enable measurements at several different electrode separations to be collected simultaneously. The combined results can provide a degree of vertical characterisation for buried features (*Figure 9*) or

Figure 8: Earth resistance devices in use. System (a) in standard twin electrode configuration; (b) with a multi-electrode array controlled by a MPX15 multiplexer (photograph courtesy of Roger Walker, Geoscan Research); (c) mounted on a MSP40 square array cart with a fluxgate gradiometer also attached; (d) the ARP© system with three electrode separations (photograph courtesy of Geocarta S.A.).

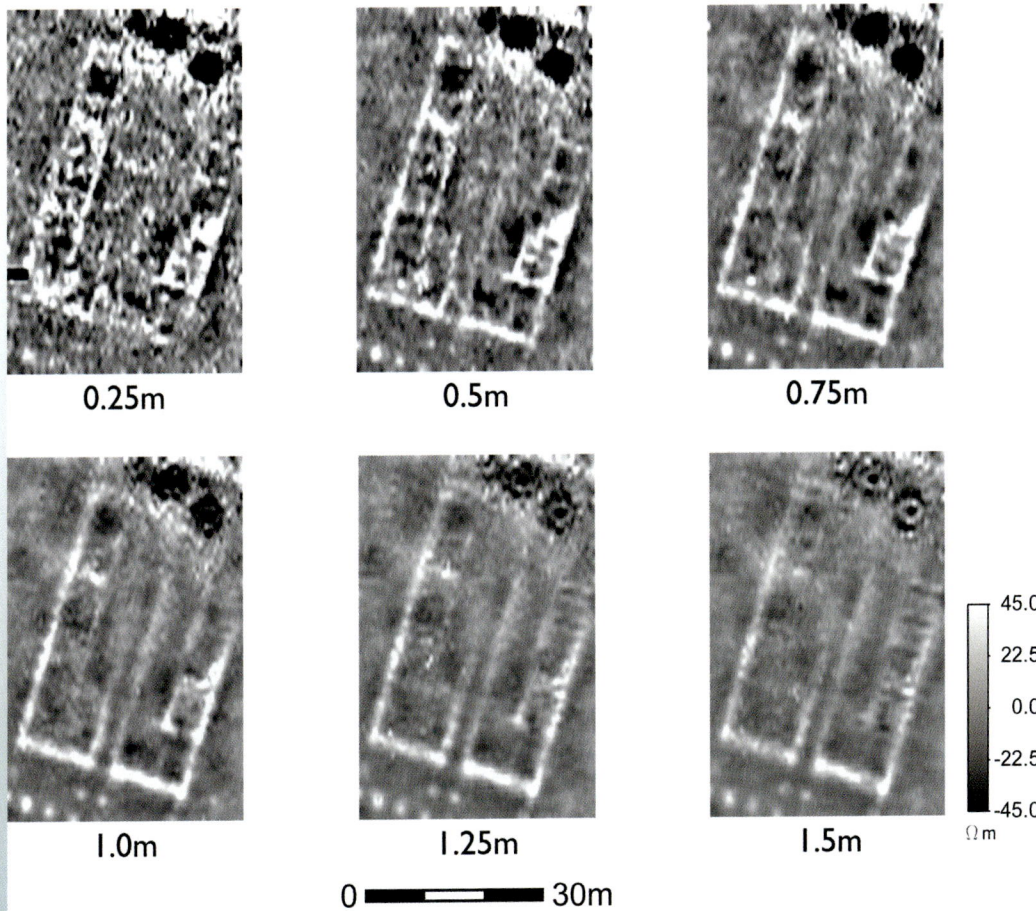

Figure 9: Earth resistance survey conducted using six different electrode separations. The data were collected over a Roman building at Wroxeter, Shropshire.
The closer separations detect near-surface features, such as the footings of internal partition walls, while the wider separations preferentially detect the footings of the external structural walls indicating that these continue to a greater depth below the surface (data courtesy of Roger Walker, Geoscan Research).

be used to filter out geological trends and accentuate near-surface archaeological features (Clark 1996).

Different geologies, soils, and variations in soil moisture, temperature and chemical content can all affect the magnitude of the earth resistance anomaly caused by a buried feature; the optimum range setting and measurement resolution will therefore usually have to be determined for each site at the time of the survey. Under typical conditions of temperate climate measurements might range between 0 and 200 Ohms in which case a resolution of 0.1 Ohm would be suitable. However, in dry conditions much higher earth resistances can be encountered and a measurement range of 0 to 2000 Ohms might be needed, in which case a resolution of 1 Ohm would be acceptable.

The maximum acceptable survey resolution for earth resistance area surveys is 1 m × 1 m and this sample density is adequate to detect (Level 1) the presence of archaeological anomalies in most circumstances. Increasing sample density to 0.5 m × 1 m or 0.5 m × 0.5m can produce sharper detail (*Figure 10*) but increases the time required to survey the area (Clark 1996), although modern multiplexed systems can minimise the additional time required. Since earth resistance methods sample a volume of ground that is determined by the electrode separation (signal convolution of an active method) a survey resolution that is smaller than the electrode separation only improves marginally the resolving power of the results (Schmidt 2013a).

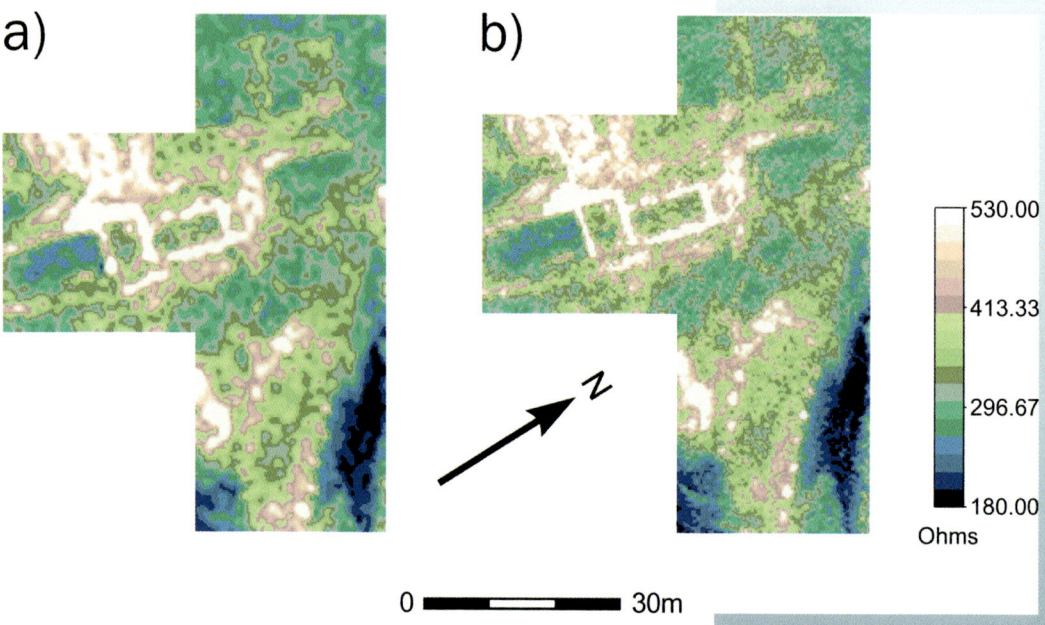

Figure 10: Earth resistance surveys at Freens Court, Herefordshire; comparison of sampling density. Sample density was (a) 1 m x 1 m and (b) 0.5 m x 0.5 m density (b), illustrating the improved resolution of the latter, which resolves two rows of discrete post pad anomalies in the eastern (bottom) part of the survey area.

Area survey with the twin-probe system involves positioning two fixed remote electrodes at a distance of some 15 m to 30 m (approximately 30 times the mobile electrode separation) from the mobile frame and connected to it by a cable. As the survey progresses it will become necessary to reposition the remote electrodes so that the survey can continue and care should be taken to level measurements between the new and old remote electrode positions to avoid discontinuities in the measured survey data (Gaffney and Gater 2003). However, changing the separation of the remote electrodes affects the contrast of the data and maintaining a fixed separation of remote

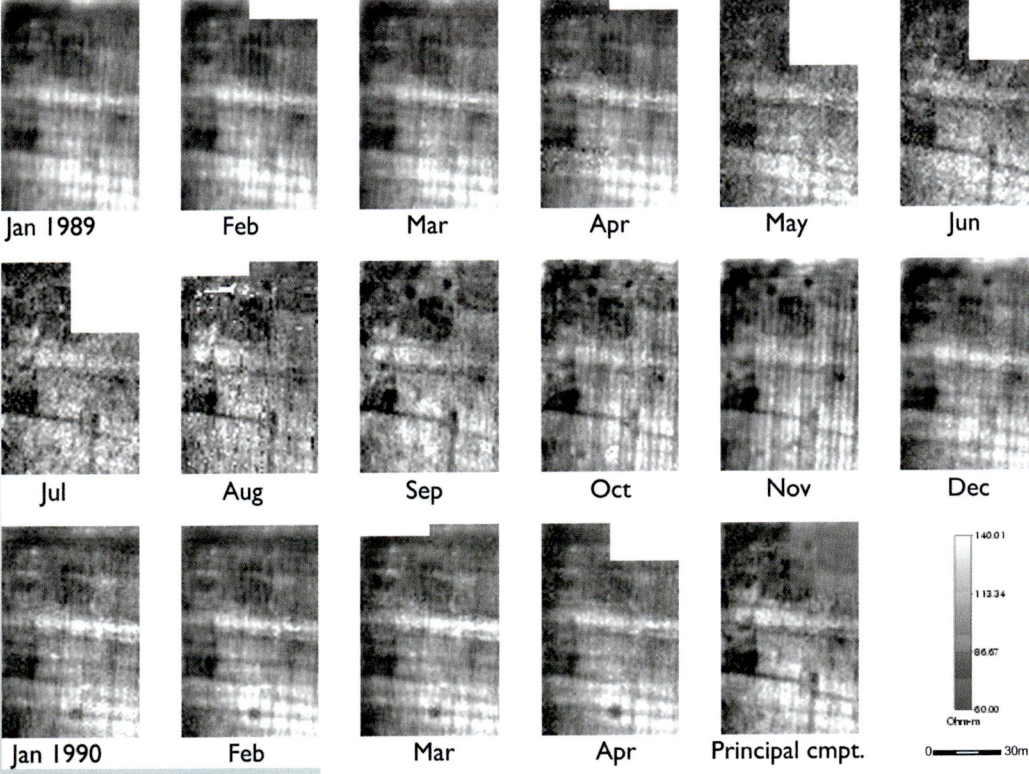

Figure 11: Earth resistance surveys over the same area at Stanwick Roman Villa, Northamptonshire repeated at monthly intervals for eighteen months. The data illustrate the seasonality of the response of archaeological features to this technique. High resistance (white) anomalies are clearest in winter when the soil has a high moisture content, while low resistance (black) anomalies are clearest in the summer months, when there is a high soil moisture deficit.

electrodes and balancing data grids subsequently by software can in some cases provide better results (Schmidt 2013a). The need for balancing may be greatly reduced, or even eliminated, by separating the remote electrodes from each other by a large distance (Dabas et al. 2000) but at the expense of maintaining a greater separation from the mobile frame (necessitating a longer cable) and increased sensitivity to electrical interference. Underground electricity cables and pipelines with cathodic corrosion protection can produce significant electrical interference and, when working in their vicinity, care should be taken to set the resistance meter's current frequency filters and measurement averaging times to ensure that a stable measurement can be achieved. Indeed, it may not be possible to survey for up to several metres either side of such underground electricity cables and pipelines.

Surveyors and their clients should of course be aware that the earth resistance response depends on moisture contrasts in the soil and that these are in turn interdependent on climatic regime, vegetation, soil and feature type. For optimum results it is necessary to take these factors into account and, preferably, to conduct the survey at a time when moisture contrasts are at their most accentuated[9] (Schmidt 2013a), or to re-survey the site at different times of year (*Figure 11* and Clark 1996; Gebbers *et al.* 2009). Regrettably, such approaches will be unrealistic within the time constraints of most development programmes; nevertheless any such limitations should be noted in the subsequent report.

1.3.4 Electrical resistivity imaging (ERI)
While earth resistance surveys are usually undertaken to cover a contiguous area of ground in two dimensions, it is also possible to generate depth sections using electrical resistivity imaging (ERI). Earth resistance measurements are most sensitive to features buried at a particular depth, which, as mentioned above, is influenced by the electrode separation of the array used. By repeating measurements at each point on the surface using a number of different electrode separations it is possible to obtain information about the variation of earth resistance with depth – a simple example using six different separations is illustrated in *Figure 9*. However, more detailed depth information may be determined by laying out a linear array of electrodes (for example 25 to 64) and connecting them to a multiplexed earth resistance meter, so that measurements at all possible separations and positions are made (electrical resistivity tomography (ERT); Milsom 2002).

In a basic ERI only a single electrode configuration is used (e.g. Wenner) albeit with varying electrode separation for each location and the results can then be visualised in a 'pseudosection' (Schmidt 2013a). By ascribing each measurement in the form of an 'apparent resistivity' to a horizontal location beneath the centre position of the four electrodes used and a depth proportional to their relative separation, an approximation of a vertical slice through the ground can be built up. Such pseudosections contain distortions resulting from the often complex interaction between the electric current flow and resistive features in the subsurface (Aspinall and Crummett 1997), but a more realistic electrical section may be created using computer post-processing with iterative inversion algorithms to calculate the estimated resistivity for all subsurface positions (see Section 2.1.3, Modelling and inversion, and Loke and Barker 1996). An example showing the use of electrical imaging to characterise buried wall footings is shown in *Figure 12*.

Electrical imaging has been employed with some success to characterise archaeological anomalies and three-dimensional surveys can be constructed by measuring a sequence of parallel sections and stacking the results (Collier *et al.* 2003; Papadopoulos *et al.* 2006). However, the technique is slow compared to area survey methods, as a large number of electrodes need to be positioned for each section. Electrical sections are therefore usually employed to improve the characterisation of anomalies that were detected by other techniques (e.g. by area survey), rather than for their initial discovery. Nevertheless, they are increasingly employed in geomorphological studies to provide details of buried landscapes associated with archaeological activity. In this application, large geological-scale sections are measured at strategically targeted locations, typically using more

---

[9] Prolonged spells of rain or drought often result in poor electrical contrast.

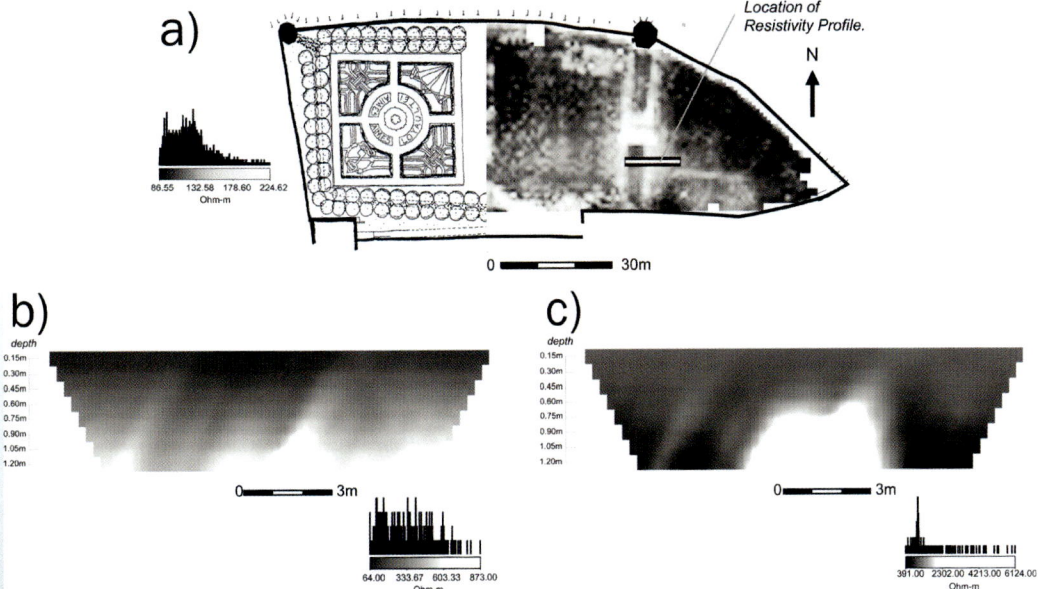

Figure 12: Earth resistance survey at Basing House, Hampshire: (a) 0.5 m twin-probe earth resistance area survey identifying a portion of the medieval curtain wall footings (strong white linear anomalies); (b) twin-probe 'pseudosection' showing the earth resistance of a vertical profile along the line indicated in (a); and (c) inversion of the data shown in (b) clearly showing the buried wall footing in cross section.

widely separated electrodes than for direct analysis of archaeological-scale anomalies (Bates and Bates 2000; Bates et al. 2007).

Where electrical sections are employed, an inter-electrode separation suited to the scale and depth of the expected anomalies should be chosen. This might be as narrow as 0.5 – 1 m when imaging archaeological features, but may be much wider (2 m, 5 m or more) for geomorphological studies. Different electrode configurations (Wenner, dipole-dipole, etc.) have different response characteristics (Loke 2004; Schmidt 2013a), so the configuration used and the reasons for its selection should be noted in the survey report. Care should also be taken to minimise the contact resistances of each electrode in the array (typically to <1000 Ohms) before initiating the measurement sequence. Most data acquisition software for electrical imaging will include a facility to test the contact resistances of each electrode. It is sometimes possible to improve the contact resistance by moistening the insertion point with water and re-inserting the respective electrode but the time variation of effects caused by the drying-out of the contact has to be monitored.

Table 2: Summary of expected GPR response over various types of sites and features.

Type of site or feature	Expected response	Comments
building remains, foundations and wall footings	good	Generally very well resolved; previous earth resistance survey may indicate sufficient conductivity contrasts.
Services	good	Modern services, particularly metal pipes, can be readily distinguished. Small-bore plastic services may be more difficult to image. More significant stone-lined drains and conduits can also be resolved.
site stratigraphy	moderate	Provided adequate physical contrast between adjacent layers and features exists, stratigraphy can be resolved within the limits of spatial resolution of the antenna (Table 3).
voids and cavities	good	The contrast between air-filled voids and surrounding soil produces a strong reflection. Distinctive polarity reversals of the incident wave form may also be discerned. Partially filled voids containing rubble or water may also be resolved.
standing structures, historic buildings	good	Specific architectural questions, such as the presence of hidden void spaces within a wall, may be resolved. High frequency antennas are often required and are effective for locating metallic features.
Wetlands	moderate/good	Response may be highly site-dependent and influenced by the presence of high-conductivity clays. Success has been reported for imaging targets in peat and below fresh water.
Geomorphology	moderate/good	Lower-frequency antenna may be required in the presence of alluvial clays, but palaeochannels and other large scale features can still be located. The depth of overburden can also be mapped.
pits, ditches, post-holes	moderate	Very site-dependent, but successful surveys have demonstrated the suitability of GPR for these feature types. Physical contrast and feature size can limit detection.
Graves	poor/moderate	Dependent on the nature of interment and depth of the feature; stone-lined coffins usually provide a strong reflector.

1.4 GROUND PENETRATING RADAR

Collectively, the term ground penetrating radar (GPR) has been applied at an administrative level within Europe to all methods of geophysical survey utilising electromagnetic radiation in a range from 30 MHz to 8 GHz to image buried structures. This encompasses a wide range of applications and the term is used here to describe the more common, commercially available GPR systems suitable for archaeological surveys (Conyers and Goodman 1997; Daniels 2004; Reynolds 1997; Vaughan 1986; Conyers 2012).

1.4.1 Choosing GPR survey

GPR can often be more costly than conventional methods of area geophysical survey (e.g. magnetic and earth resistance techniques), but does present some unique capabilities to provide estimates of the depth to target features and, under suitable conditions, present three-dimensional models of buried remains. GPR can also be the only practical method to apply on certain sites, or within standing buildings, where the presence of hard surfaces and above-ground ferrous disturbance precludes the use of other geophysical techniques. However, the resolution of vertical stratigraphy is limited by, and highly dependent on the site conditions and the instrumentation deployed.

A wide range of site surfaces may be considered for GPR survey, including concrete, tarmac and even fresh water, although the technique is limited by the attenuation of the signal in conductive media. In practice, this will be determined largely by the concentration of clay and the moisture content of the soil at the site. Highly conductive media, such as metal objects or salt water will prove mostly opaque to the GPR signal. Strong reflectors in the near-surface will also reduce the energy transmitted to immediately underlying targets and this may include the local water table (or other near-surface interfaces). Ferrous reinforcement bars in concrete are also readily imaged by GPR but their presence may preclude the identification of underlying reflectors, depending on the GPR frequency used.

For normal ground-coupled antenna, good physical contact with the site surface is necessary to ensure adequate coupling of the radar energy into the soil. As far as possible, vegetation and any other surface obstructions should be removed from the site prior to the survey. High-frequency, air-launched horn antennas are designed to be operated from above the ground surface for civil engineering applications (e.g. road deck investigations), but do not usually have sufficient depth penetration for archaeological surveys. Air-launched antennas may prove useful for surveying delicate architectural features (e.g. plaster mouldings, wall paintings or mosaic pavements) when it is desirable to avoid physical contact between the instrument and the surface under investigation and where the features are buried at shallow depth. Wide bandwidth air-launched antenna arrays are also available and have been tested, with varying degrees of success, for archaeological applications (Linford *et al.* 2010; Leckebusch 2011).

Many site-specific variables have to be considered when using GPR, but in general it will respond to a wide range of archaeological features (Table 2), and is often successful over sites where earth resistance survey has proved fruitful (e.g. presence of masonry walls, void spaces, etc). GPR responds to the interfaces between differing materials and some target features produce highly distinctive GPR anomalies (e.g. hyperbolic responses from point reflectors). However, the identification of complex material properties, for example distinguishing either human or animal bone from the surrounding substrate, is considered to be currently beyond the capabilities of the technique under typical field conditions.

Accurate depth estimation from GPR surveys is often hard to achieve due to the difficulties in obtaining the actual electromagnetic ground velocity (see Section 1.4.5, Methodology - Detailed area survey), yet is a critical process for the successful presentation and interpretation of results. Unprocessed GPR data, expressed in terms of the time delay of returned reflections ('two-way-travel time'), can usually be calibrated to a depth scale in the light of additional information to present a physical depth estimate for the detected anomalies. An estimate for the accuracy of such conversion should always be provided.

While the use of GPR for detailed large area surveys has increased in recent years (Gaffney *et al.* 2012) it is currently often applied as a complementary technique, following the acquisition of magnetic or earth resistance data, to target specific archaeological anomalies identified over a more limited area of the site. Care must be taken to ensure that GPR survey is appropriate to a site, particularly if it is the only technique to be applied. The proximity to sources of radio-frequency (RF) interference that may affect the data quality – such as mobile telephone transmitter base stations or the radio modem of an on-site differential GPS/GNSS system – should be considered. Even a simple mobile phone near the investigated area may emit sufficient electromagnetic radiation to disturb the data.

1.4.2 Instrumentation

Most GPR systems utilise an electromagnetic pulse, generated by a transmitter antenna on the ground surface, and record the amplitude and time delay of any reflections from buried structures. These reflections are produced when the GPR pulse is incident upon any media with contrasting dielectric *permittivity* (ε) to the medium above. Under certain circumstances a contrast in electrical *conductivity* (σ) may also influence the reflection. The *magnetic permeability* (μ) of the sub-surface will also influence the propagation of a radar wave, but for most archaeological applications is of little influence. In practice, the GPR response will be largely determined by the local variation of water content in the sub-surface. The maximum depth of penetration for a GPR is governed by a combination of signal scattering and attenuation within the subsurface, through the dissipation of radio-frequency energy as eddy currents within conductive media.

The majority of archaeological materials and soils reflect only part of the GPR signal and allow the remainder to be transmitted further downwards so that the electromagnetic waves can penetrate to some depth, creating a series of secondary reflections from objects and interfaces buried deeper; distinguished by an increasing time delay. The resulting time-amplitude data are displayed as a two-dimensional profile with the x-axis indicating the horizontal location of the antenna on the ground surface and the y-axis representing the increasing time delay (related to depth) from the initial impulse. While radar waves propagate more slowly in the ground than in the air, velocities are still extremely high (near speed of light) and the receiver electronics is capable of recording events separated by less than a nanosecond (10^{-9} s). The recorded delay represents the total time required for an incident pulse to travel from the transmitter to the target and then for the reflection to return to the receiver. This dual pathway is known as a *two-way travel time* and can often be converted to provide the approximate depth of buried targets where an accurate estimate of the sub-surface velocity can be made (see Section 1.4.5, Methodology - Detailed area survey).

Most GPR systems consist of an antenna unit housing the transmitter and receiver, an electronic control unit, a data console and a power supply. Different configurations of these components are offered by the major manufacturers and each may have advantages in particular survey conditions (*Figure 13*). It is now common practice to house as many components in one casing as possible (e.g. electronic control unit, power supply and data console).

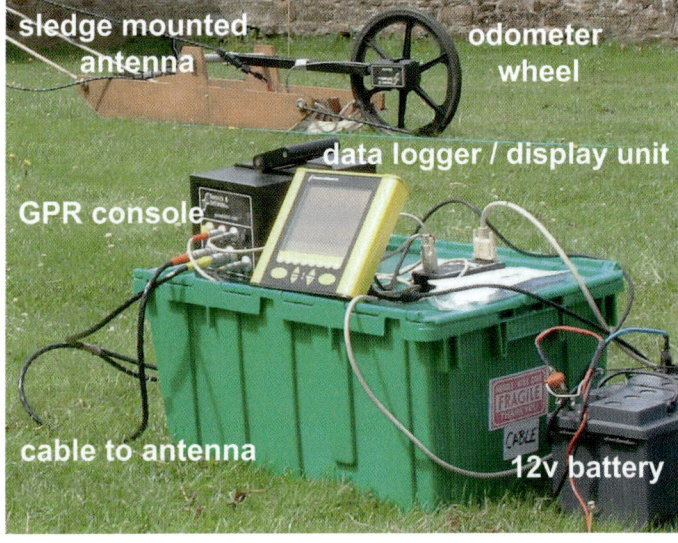

Figure 13: Annotated photograph of a Sensors and Software Pulse Ekko 1000 GPR system.
The sledge accommodates either a 900 MHz, 450 MHz or 225 MHz centre frequency antenna and maintains good coupling with the ground surface through its flexible plastic skid plate.

Antenna units

The GPR impulse covers a comparatively broad band of frequencies, usually defined by a nominal 'centre frequency'. Because of the increased attenuation of higher frequencies, low-centre-frequency antennas will provide a greater depth of penetration. However, the longer wavelengths produced by low-centre-frequency antennas will reduce the vertical and lateral resolution of buried targets and only physically large structures will be resolved at depth (Table 3). Higher frequency antennas can resolve smaller features but have less depth penetration. The footprint of the subsurface illuminated by the approximately conical spreading of radar energy in the ground is frequency-dependent and increases with depth (Annan and Cosway 1992, and *Figure 14*). This may limit the effective depth of investigation for certain targets and also introduce reflections from objects buried to either side of the instrument's traverse.

The majority of commercial GPR systems allow operation with a number of interchangeable antenna units with different centre frequencies to suit the soil conditions, depth of penetration and resolution required. For near-surface archaeological surveys a bistatic antenna unit, consisting of a separate transmitter and receiver component will be used, although these may be enclosed within a common housing. Most mid- to high-centre-frequency antennas will also be shielded to minimise unwanted reflections from above-ground targets (e.g. cars). More specialised antenna units designed for specific requirements such as borehole surveys or high-frequency air-launched systems for road pavement analysis are also available.

Electronic control unit

These units provide the driving signal to the antenna and sample the received response at a sufficiently high frequency. Modern systems digitise the receiver data directly, enabling detailed post-acquisition processing. Some units may apply an analogue gain directly to the

Table 3: Approximate values for the variation of GPR penetration depth and resolution with centre frequency
The estimates are provided for typical soils, encompassing a range of values for relative dielectric permittivity ('dielectric constant') and soil conductivities. The horizontal resolution will decrease with depth and is given for the maximum penetration depth, assuming a relative dielectric permittivity ε_r = 15. These values are intended as a guide and can be recalculated based on a more detailed estimate of the site conditions and target parameters.

Centre Frequency (MHz)	Depth penetration for typical soils (m)	Wavelength (λ) in soil ε_r = 15 (m)	Horizontal resolution – width of Fresnel zone at maximum depth (m)	Vertical resolution $\lambda/4$ (m)
1000	ca. 1.0	0.08	0.2	0.02
500	ca. 2.0	0.16	0.4	0.04
200	ca. 3.0	0.39	0.8	0.10
100	ca. 5.0	0.77	1.4	0.19
50	ca. 7.0	1.55	2.4	0.39

Vertical resolution   *Horizontal resolution*

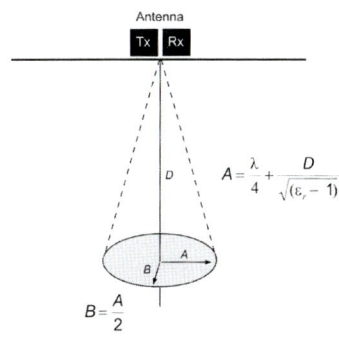

$$f_c > \frac{75}{\Delta Z \sqrt{\varepsilon_r}} \text{ MHz}$$

signal prior to digitisation, to improve the discrimination of later reflections, but it is important to avoid clipping the response beyond the maximum amplitude value recorded by the system. Older analogue instruments, producing only a graphical record of the GPR traces, are not appropriate for archaeological surveys because it is not possible to apply any post-acquisition processing or visualisation to the data.

Increasingly, GPR systems offer multi-channel operation where data from two or more sets of antennas can be recorded simultaneously. This might allow a site to be covered with a range of centre frequencies, imaging both near-surface and deeper-lying targets, or a parallel array of antenna units can be used for the rapid acquisition of densely sampled data.

Data console
The function of the data console is to set the instrument parameters on the control unit, to view the receiver output in real time and to record the digitised data securely. A laptop computer running suitable control software can often suffice for this purpose, using an internal hard disk drive for data storage and a high speed transport bus to cope with the large volume of data produced by the GPR system. Integration with a co-located GPS/GNSS receiver or robotic EDM enables the simultaneous collection of positional and topographic data (e.g. Leckebusch 2005).

Figure 14: The vertical and horizontal resolution of a GPR system are determined by the antenna.
They can be estimated from the antenna's centre frequency (fc) and the relative dielectric permittivity (ε_r) of the ground from which the wavelength (λ) can be derived. The 'footprint' of the conically spreading energy increases with depth (D) reducing the effective horizontal resolution (figure adapted from Annan and Cosway 1992).

Power supply
GPR systems require a reliable power supply to function adequately throughout the working day. In the past this power was supplied from a 12 V lead acid battery but modern systems use sealed high energy density batteries or are powered directly from a vehicle.

System mounting
Integrated GPR systems have been designed for single user operation with all of the components mounted on a compact, collapsible wheeled cart. These systems are readily portable and may be deployed on sites where the absence of trailing cables between the various subunits can greatly speed up the rate of data acquisition. However, where antennas have to be operated very close to obstacles, modular systems may offer some benefits. Transport of the antenna units may be improved by mounting these on a sledge with a flexible plastic skid to ride over uneven terrain while maintaining good coupling with the ground surface. A GPR system usually includes an odometer wheel to automatically trigger the unit at set distance intervals; these require calibration when operated over sites with uneven terrain.

1.4.3 Continuous-wave radar
The majority of commercial ground penetrating radar instruments utilise an impulse source to introduce energy into the ground. This limits both the potential bandwidth of transmitted signal and the ability to couple energy effectively with the ground surface. These problems may be overcome by the use of a continuous source, either swept (frequency-modulated continuous wave) or held at a series of steps (synthesised or stepped-frequency) over a range of transmitter frequencies, although the received signal requires more involved processing (Linford *et al.* 2010; Leckebusch 2011).

Somers *et al.* (2005) demonstrate an alternative approach to continuous-wave radio-frequency imaging by introducing a source transmitter beneath the intended target through a small-diameter borehole. The energy from the buried source then passes back up to the ground surface having been modified, in terms of both amplitude and phase, by the illuminated archaeological features. These variations are recorded by a mobile receiver over the site surface and may be processed with appropriate reconstruction algorithms. The reconstruction algorithm can be adjusted to focus the resulting image on a particular depth of the target beneath the surface.

1.4.4 Methodology
This section considers only the use of impulse GPR operating in a *common offset* antenna configuration (i.e. where the separation between transmitter and receiver antenna is fixed).

Initial field tests are recommended to confirm that the equipment is functioning as expected, and that instrument parameters are correctly set. Antennas of differing centre frequencies could be trialled to determine an appropriate balance between resolution and depth of penetration (*Figure 15*). Operators should ensure that mobile telephones and any other radio-frequency (RF) transmitters in the immediate vicinity of an impulse

GPR antenna are switched off. The survey may have to be conducted with more than one centre frequency of antenna, either because of rapidly changing site conditions (e.g. an increasing depth of overburden) or the need to resolve targets of differing physical size and depth of burial (e.g. on a deeply stratified urban site).

If the instrument trials prove unsuccessful, or suggest low data quality, then the survey should be aborted at a pre-agreed fee. This may be unnecessary for small surveys, where data acquisition is unlikely to exceed a single day in the field.

The requirement for a survey grid is similar to other geophysical techniques discussed above, but operation on standing buildings may impose special requirements for recording the position of the antenna over the face of a wall or ceiling. It is often best to align survey transects parallel to any surface irregularities, for example kerb stones, to maintain good antenna coupling with the ground along each transect.

Very strong above-ground radar reflectors (e.g. metal fences, metal walls or large vehicles) next to the survey area may produce spurious reflections in the data even for shielded antennas, caused by energy leaking from the transmitter and being reflected back to some extent into the receiver – no shielding is perfect. A similar effect may also occur over sites with uneven terrain where the antennas do not always make good physical contact with

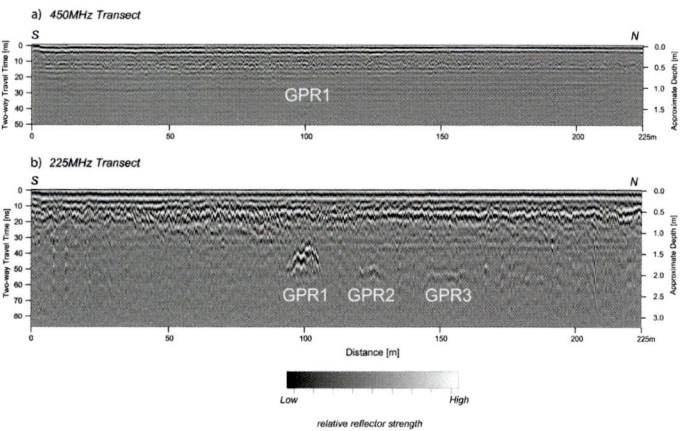

Figure 15: Trial GPR transect collected over peaty soil repeated with 450 MHz (a) and 225 MHz (b) centre frequency antennas. At this site the lower frequency antenna has successfully identified three deeply buried anomalies that are only partially visible in the higher frequency data.

the ground surface. Such *air wave* anomalies can be distinguished in the data as having characteristically high velocity (approximately 0.3 m/ns) and being of limited attenuation compared with sub-surface reflectors. Near-surface horizontal reflectors, such as concrete surfaces or metal manhole covers, may cause the incident radar pulse to reverberate repeatedly between the antenna and the surface, resulting in high amplitude multiple reflections ('ringing') down the profile.

There are three main modes of GPR data acquisition:

Scanning
GPR instruments provide a real-time visual display of the measured data and may be used to locate known or suspected features, perhaps during invasive works in the field. Cart-based systems may be reversed along the survey line automatically scrolling the data backwards to identify the location of an anomaly. While this may be useful for an initial overview of a site, it cannot be used as a survey technique as the data are not recorded. As with magnetometer scanning, this is not a recommended strategy for archaeological prospecting.

Individual recorded profiles
Single profiles may be recorded over the suspected location of known features or to investigate anomalies identified by other geophysical techniques; for example, to estimate the depth to a particular target or to determine the course of a linear feature over an extensive area where the route may be estimated between more widely spaced traverses. However, a wide separation of such individual profiles would lead to a very low effective spatial resolution (see Part I, 3.4) and requires specific justification.

Detailed area survey
Area survey over a regular grid of closely spaced traverses is strongly recommended for detailed GPR investigations. Ideally, to avoid spatial aliasing, traverse separation should be less than the approximate footprint of the radar energy at the required depth of investigation (*Figure 14* and Table 3). Under typical conditions for a 500 MHz centre-frequency antenna any traverse separation wider than 0.25m will result in insufficiently sampled data. Only where the shape of archaeological features is of less interest may wider traverse separations be used (e.g. 0.5 m). This, however, would be negating some of the benefits of GPR survey.

The non-symmetric radiation pattern from a GPR antenna causes the orientation of targets – with respect to the direction of the profile – to influence the anomaly produced. Repeat survey over orthogonal traverses may account for this but makes subsequent data integration fairly complex. A closer separation of survey transects (e.g. 0.125 m, which takes less time than a second orthogonal survey) usually is sufficient to detect features even with problematic reflection patterns (e.g. Conyers 2004). Profiles collected over a regular grid may be acquired in either a parallel (uni-directional) or zigzag (bi-directional) manner, providing sufficient care is taken with the positioning of the antenna's actual centre to avoid any shift between alternate lines.

The resulting data can be presented as a series of *time slices* where each successive time slice represents the quasi-horizontal variation of reflected energy across the survey area for a given two-way travel time interval. Visualising the GPR results in this format can greatly assist with the interpretation of complex data-sets (although some types of anomalies, for example from dipping reflectors passing through several time slices, may not be adequately resolved). Additional modes of display and data analysis, including examination of individual profiles, are recommended to help with the analysis of the time slices. For example, data-ringing can easily be detected in GPR profiles but may appear as an extended depth extent in time slices. The use of three-dimensional representations of the data, such as cut-away solid models iso-volumes or polygon representations (Schmidt and Tsetskhladze 2013), may enhance the visualisation of certain data-sets or anomalies, but should not be used as the sole method of visualisation

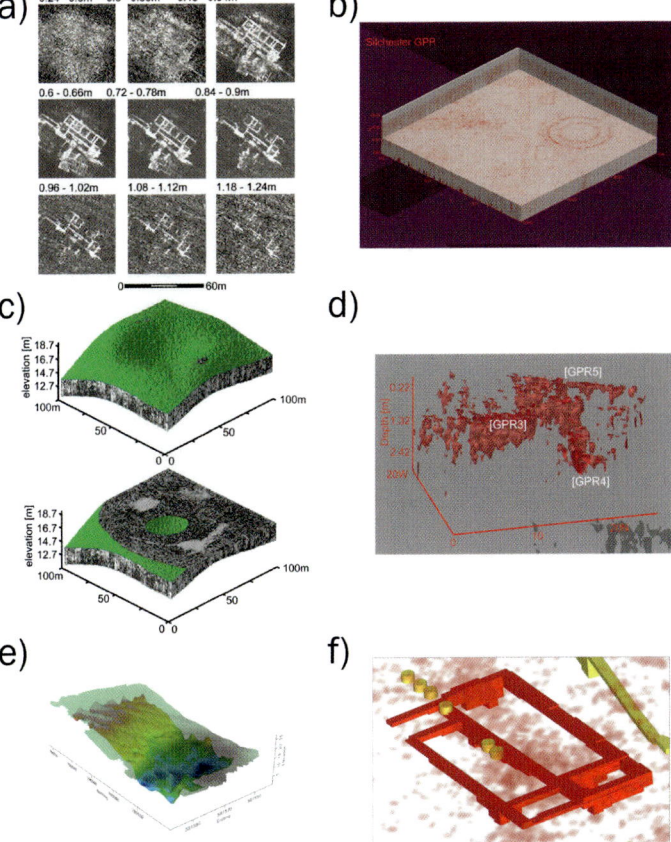

Figure 16: Examples of modes of display for three-dimensional GPR data. (a) time slices showing the variation of reflector amplitude at selected depths; (b) cut-away false perspective view of the whole data volume; (c) topographically corrected data volume showing underlying anomalies (greyscale); (d) iso-volume representation of stone-lined passages leading in to a souterrain feature; (e) buried land surface across a dry valley extracted from the GPR data beneath the (semi-transparent) DTM; and (f) a volumetric interpretation of a Roman building abstracted from time slice data overlaid with a cloud of plough damaged material.

(e.g. Leckebusch 2003; Linford 2004). *Figure 16* provides examples of various means of GPR data display.

The number of traces (scans) to be recorded along each profile, the time window through which reflections are measured for each trace and the number of times each trace is repeated at a particular sample point (stacking), should be set to appropriate values to image the targets under investigation. Due to the low signal-to-noise ratio of the GPR signal, over-sampling is recommended where this does not adversely slow data acquisition. For a typical archaeological survey, with a mid-centre-frequency antenna (500 MHz), traces should be recorded at least every 0.05 m along a profile. An increased trace density may be appropriate for more detailed survey with a higher-frequency antenna. Establishing the correct time window through field trials is also important as this will determine the maximum depth to which the GPR unit will record data.

Any time-to-depth estimate should be supported with details of how the sub-surface electromagnetic velocity was determined and applied to the data, taking into account any significant alteration of soil type across the site or variation in moisture conditions that may occur during the course of the survey. This may be achieved through either calibration between a recorded reflection and a known-depth target, analysis of the shapes of diffraction hyperbolas, common mid-point (CMP) measurements made in the field with separable transmitter- and receiver antennas (*Figure 17*) or direct determination using time-domain reflectometry of the soil.

Most GPR acquisition assumes that the profiles are collected over a planar surface. Where significant topographic variation exists this should be recorded and an appropriate elevation correction applied to the GPR data. Under conditions of gently undulating terrain (greater than ±0.5 m) the elevation correction may be applied directly to the GPR profile as a static shift to each trace (taking the electromagnetic velocity into account). However, more severe gradients will also require a tilt-angle correction to be applied to the data to avoid discrepancies in the apparent location of subsurface reflectors (e.g. Goodman *et al.* 2006; Leckebusch and Rychener 2007). The degree of horizontal displacement will depend on the slope angle of the surface and the depth of investigation. For example, anomalies identified at a depth of 1 m below a slope inclined by 20º will be shifted horizontally by approximately 0.34 m from the surface location of the GPR antenna. After determining the spatial distribution of electromagnetic velocities across the survey area the data can also be used to generate truly horizontal depth slices.

Detailed GPR survey will create large volumes of data that will initially be stored on the internal hard disk of the data console or laptop computer. However, data back-up at regular intervals to suitable high-volume secondary storage media is very important to avoid data loss.

Results from a GPR survey, whether visualised as an individual profile or as a horizontal time slice, should indicate the time delay and include an appropriate greyscale or colour key to show the variation in the amplitude of the reflections. The recommended sub-unit for the two-way travel time delay is the nanosecond (ns) and the amplitude of the reflections will initially be recorded as a potential measured by the receiver antenna in the millivolt range, although results following post-acquisition processing are generally presented in arbitrary, relative units. As they are derived from the data reflected back into the receiver antenna these are sometimes also referred to as reflection strength.

1.4.5 Radio licensing and emissions legislation
Owing to the increased demand for wireless communications and the need to avoid interference between electronic equipment, legislation has been introduced governing the use of the radio spectrum and electromagnetic compatibility (EMC) issues, or is currently under development at both a national and international level. GPR equipment must, obviously, adhere to the relevant legislation, but presents some unique considerations that do not readily fall into common categories of other similar electronic devices, such as cellular telephones or computer equipment.

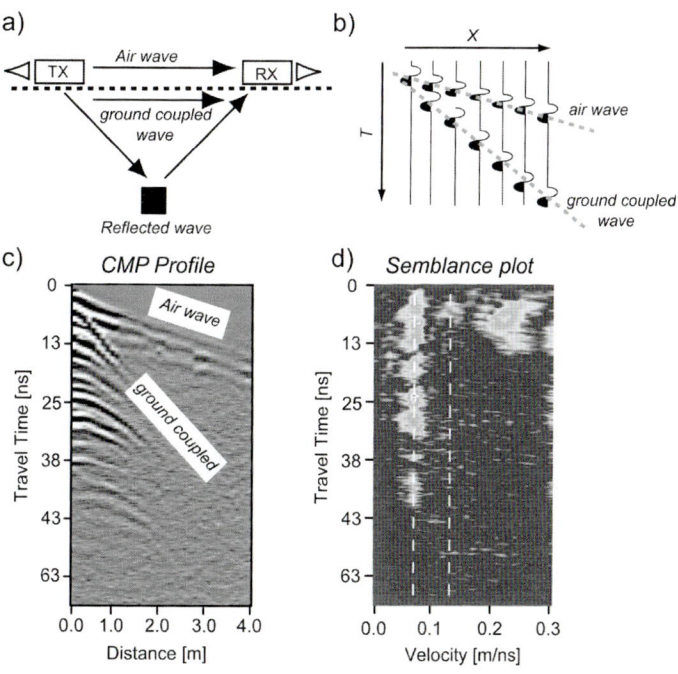

Figure 17: An estimate of the average subsurface velocity (v) can be obtained by conducting a common mid-point (CMP) survey in the field.
(a) The distance (X), between the GPR transmitter and receiver is gradually enlarged about a central point increasing (b) the two-way travel time (T) of both the air wave passing directly between the two and the ground coupled wave travelling through the very near surface, and any reflections, if present, from more deeply buried objects. The velocity of the waves can be determined from (c) the slope of the reflections on a CMP profile, which can be further enhanced by the use of (d) semblance analysis. In this case the velocity of the reflected waves from buried objects is approximately 0.075 m/ns, slightly slower than the ground coupled wave (approximately 0.125 m/ns).

Impulse GPR systems use a mobile, ultra-wide band (UWB) transmitter operating at a low-power output that is specifically designed to emit this energy into an absorptive earth-material medium, typically the ground. For archaeological applications of GPR this radiated energy generally falls between 30 MHz and 8 GHz, a portion of the radio spectrum that for administrative purposes is currently subject to legislation at a European level through standards set by the technical authority of the European Telecommunications Standards Institute (ETSI). All GPR equipment must be CE marked in order to demonstrate compliance with the European Radio and Telecommunications Terminal Equipment (R&TTE) directive 1999/5/EC (European Commission 1999) and the European directives on stray emissions (EN302 066 01 & 02). It is the duty of the manufacturer to ensure that equipment conforms to European legislation on stray emissions; self declaration by the users of the equipment is not possible. In addition, some European countries also require an operator license and all GPR users should conform to the European Code of Practice (European Telecommunications Standards Institute (ETSI) Guidance document ETSI EG 202 730 http://bit.ly/1kI85ll, which is based on EuroGPR's Code of Practice http://bit.ly/Rk0rFe). This also requires the use of a site log for operation (see www.eurogpr.org for more details). Equipment rental pools will record site log details and licensing arrangements for occasional users hiring GPR instruments.

Generally, the areas of most concern with regards to EMC are:
- airfields;
- prisons;
- defence establishments, including military training grounds; and
- radio astronomy sites.

Most recently manufactured GPR equipment will have been designed to meet current EMC legislation and operate at a lower power than previous comparable instruments. These requirements also permit the operation of wide-band pulse techniques. Advances in antenna design and integral electronics often result in these modern systems surpassing the performance, in terms of depth penetration and signal-to-noise ratio, of the earlier generation of instruments that they have replaced (e.g. Sirri *et al.* 2005).

Additional concerns for the GPR user community are:

- operation beyond the agreed bandwidth (150 and 4000 MHz for the U.K. Frequency Allocation Table);
- compliance of older legacy equipment with new regulations;
- restrictions on the development of future equipment; and
- transmission surveys / vertical faces (control of energy absorption).

1.5 LOW-FREQUENCY ELECTROMAGNETIC METHODS

A range of geophysical instruments make use of electromagnetic (EM) fields and waves, distinguished by the frequency and duration of the source that they utilise. While such a broad definition includes GPR (using high-frequency EM waves), magnetic susceptibility meters and metal detectors, these special cases are discussed individually elsewhere. This section therefore considers only low-frequency EM (LFEM) instruments with transmitter- and receiver coils separated by a fixed distance, also known as 'Slingram' devices. As they were in the past mainly used to measure ground conductivity they are also sometimes, somewhat misleadingly, referred to as electromagnetic induction devices (EMI). These continuously generate EM fields that vary with a low-frequency (<300 kHz) in the transmitter coil, that will in turn generate secondary fields within electrical conductors or magnetic features present in the near-surface ground (e.g. Wait 1955). A separate tuned receiver coil records these secondary signals emitted from subsurface structures. It is found that the in-phase component is largely proportional to the magnetic susceptibility of the subsurface and the out of phase, or quadrature, response mostly to the electrical conductivity. Theoretically, as conductivity is the reciprocal of resistivity, this modulated signal enables an EM instrument to simultaneously collect data-sets comparable to both the earth resistance and the (induced) magnetic response (e.g. fluxgate gradiometer survey) from a site.

Initial research had already demonstrated the ability of EM instruments to identify archaeological features (e.g. Scollar 1962; Tabbagh 1986; Tite and Mullins 1969), and the technique has recently been used more widely, with very encouraging results (De Smedt et al. 2013b). As the coils of an EM instrument do not have to make contact with the ground surface they offer the advantage of rapid field data acquisition, combined with the simultaneous collection of conductivity and magnetic data-sets[10]. However, considerable inter-site variability of the EM response may be encountered, depending on underlying geology and soils, requiring calibration against more conventional methods of geophysical survey. EM instruments are also sensitive to conductive objects in the near-surface that may preclude their use on some sites, for example metal fences, rubbish, buried pipes, etc, and to electrical interference from both cultural (e.g. power lines) and atmospheric sources.

For most archaeological applications an EM instrument with an inter-coil separation of approximately 1 m will suffice (*Figure 18*), but instruments with several coil separations are now available that allow to record simultaneously data from different depths. Field operation and calibration will vary between instruments, but it is possible to convert the recorded signal (often expressed as parts per thousand or ppt) to units of apparent conductivity in milli-Siemens per metre (mS/m) and volume specific magnetic susceptibility (dimensionless). The effective depth of penetration is largely dependent on the separation between the transmitter and receiver coils, analogous to expanding the electrodes of an earth resistance array, although the physical orientation of the coils allows

---

[10] The conductivity data-sets from most currently available LFEM systems are of considerable better quality than the magnetic data-sets due to the challenges inherent in the instrument design.

even an instrument with one fixed separation to provide a shallow and a deeper penetrating mode of operation (e.g. Keller and Frischknecht 1966). Comparative studies with instruments such as the Geonics EM38 demonstrate a good correlation with twin-probe earth resistance and magnetic surveys (*Figure 19*; Cole *et al.* 1995; Huang and Won 2000; Kvamme 2003). However, certain combinations of site conditions, coil orientation, operating frequency and phase may produce a complex signal that is not directly proportional to a single physical property of the sub-surface (e.g. Linford 1998; Tabbagh 1986; Tite and Mullins 1973).

More widely spaced traverses may be of use when a deeper penetrating (wider coil separation) instrument is used to identify geomorphological features, such as palaeochannels, or map changes of soil magnetic susceptibility across an expansive landscape. Rates of coverage will vary depending on the precise instrument and sample interval in use, but should be similar to earth resistance. Vehicle-mounted instruments with integrated GPS/GNSS measurements are more rapid and enable several hectares to be covered in a day (Saey *et al.* 2012).

Figure 18: Compact EM instruments with an inter-coil separation of 1 m are well suited to archaeological surveys.
(a) hand operated Geonics EM38B (14.6 kHz) with integrated GPS, recording both conductivity and magnetic properties of the subsurface;
(b) deeper penetrating Geonics EM31 (9.8 kHz) with a 3 m coil separation mounted onboard the GEEP multi-instrument sledge system together with two towed EM38 instruments (photograph courtesy Ian Hill, University of Leicester);
(c) trailer mounted DualEM 421S allowing 6 different depth measurements simultaneously (photograph courtesy Geocarta S.A.).

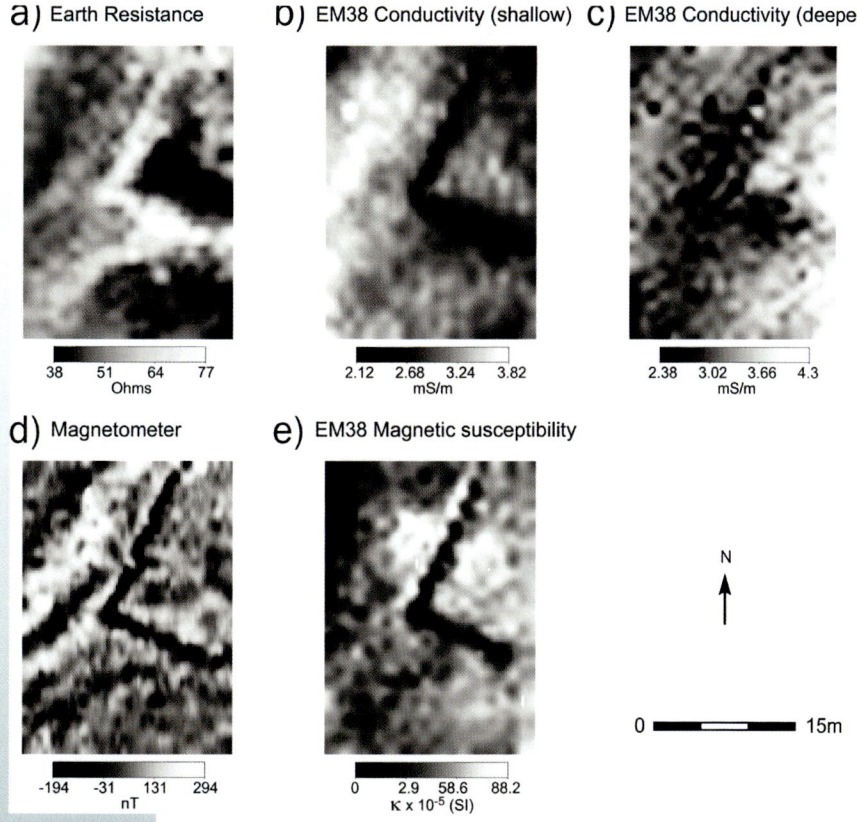

Figure 19: Comparison between different survey techniques over a buried Roman wall.
(a) twin-probe earth resistance data collected with a 0.5 m mobile electrode separation; conductivity data collected with a Geonics EM38 in shallow (horizontal) (b) and deeper penetrating (vertical) (c) coil orientations; (d) fluxgate magnetometer data; (e) in-phase, vertical coil orientation, EM magnetic susceptibility data.

1.6 TOPSOIL MAGNETIC SUSCEPTIBILITY SURVEY

Archaeological settlement activity often results in a localised concentration of soils and sediments with an enhanced magnetic susceptibility, because of the alteration of naturally occurring iron minerals (Clark 1983; Clark 1996; Cole *et al.* 1995; Dalan and Banerjee 1998; Evans and Heller 2003; Fassbinder and Stanjek 1993; Linford 2005; Thompson and Oldfield 1986). Measurements are generally made in the field (although soil samples may be recovered for laboratory determination) at a coarse sample interval of 5 m (for a coarse Level 1 investigation (Prospection) this may be increased to 10 m), utilising suitable instrumentation (*Figure 20* and *Figure 21*). Care should be taken to account for the presence of masking deposits, the influence of recent land use and field conditions at the time of the survey that may reduce the contact between a field coil and the ground surface. Laboratory determination may allow more detailed sample preparation and additional measurements (e.g. frequency dependence of susceptibility or fractional conversion). Units of volume specific magnetic susceptibility (κ) used for measurements made with a field loop are dimensionless within the SI system and laboratory determination from recovered soil samples should be corrected to values of mass specific magnetic susceptibility (χ) in dimensions of m^3kg^{-1}.

Usually, a wider survey extending beyond the evaluation study area should be considered, to allow any regional correlation between magnetic susceptibility with geology and soil type to be distinguished from possible anthropogenic enhancement (e.g. Dearing *et al.* 1996, Fig. 1). Even under ideal field conditions topsoil magnetic susceptibility survey remains an indicative technique that is unable to establish the definitive presence, or absence, of archaeological remains without the support of additional methods of evaluation. Topsoil magnetic susceptibility survey alone is, therefore, not recommended and evidence of an indifferent response to this technique should not be used to discount the potential presence of archaeological features. The comparatively greater influence of ground surface conditions and masking deposits such as alluvium create anomalous areas of both increased and depleted topsoil magnetic susceptibility and should therefore always be investigated through subsequent detailed magnetometer survey.

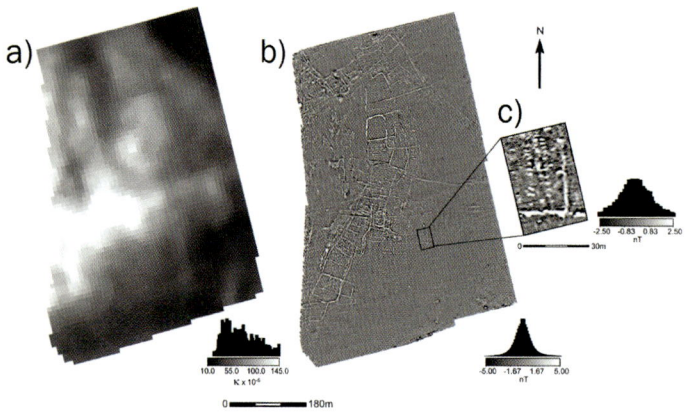

Figure 20: Area magnetic susceptibility survey. (a) showing increased response over an area of dense magnetometer anomalies (b). Low responses to the NE correlate with recent soil dumping, but some finer detail is not represented, such as a cemetery (c).

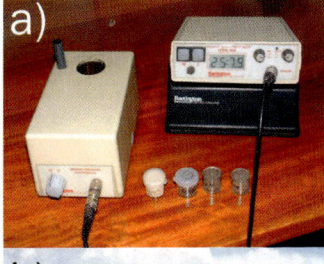

Figure 21: Bartington MS2 magnetic susceptibility meter in use.
(a) in the laboratory with collected 10 g soil samples and;
(b) on site with a field coil.

Careful consideration should always be given to the benefits of total coverage by detailed magnetometer survey, as the enhanced level of interpretation drawn from the results may often outweigh the increased costs involved. However, topsoil magnetic susceptibility results are considered to be of value when either interpreting magnetometer data (e.g. *Figure 20*), or when assessing the suitability of varying soil types and geology in advance of conducting a detailed survey. Topsoil susceptibility measurements over stripped excavation surfaces and sectioned features have also proved to be useful at an intra-site level (e.g. Bayley *et al.* 2001, Fig. 5; Linford 2003; Linford and Welch 2004), and borehole measurements have been used to determine successfully significant anomalies beneath surface deposits across wider landscapes (e.g. Dalan and Banerjee 1996).

1.7 OTHER GEOPHYSICAL METHODS

Despite offering limited use for traditional applications of archaeological evaluation a wide range of additional geophysical techniques is available that may, under certain conditions, be applicable. Some of the techniques discussed in this section are highly specific – for example the use of micro-gravity for the detection of buried voids – while other techniques propose new means for obtaining data-sets comparable with more traditional methods. Most of these latter techniques are currently at a stage of development between research and full commercial deployment, but may well be adopted as the technology matures in the near future. While the techniques discussed below would not be recommended generally, on specific sites they may find a particular application where other methods fail.

1.7.1 Capacitative arrays

These systems are designed for the rapid acquisition of apparent resistivity data and use a series of flat electrodes mounted on individual insulating mats that may be towed across a site without the need to obtain a direct contact with the ground surface (Flageul *et al.* 2013). The electric potential produced by the charges on the electrodes causes the movement of charged particles in the ground resulting in a brief capacitative coupling, continuing only until an equal and opposite reverse potential has been established in the subsurface. Use of a sufficiently high frequency source will reverse the flow of charged particles in the ground, producing an alternating current in the subsurface. Similar dipolar pairs of insulated electrodes are then used to measure the potential created by the currents in the ground.

Multiple potential electrodes can be towed at different separations behind the current electrodes to measure simultaneously the apparent resistivity at varying depths and can be numerically processed ('inverted') to provide a pseudosection of the ground surface (see Section 1.3.4, Electrical resistivity imaging (ERI)). However, at higher source frequencies, attenuation of the signal may prove to be a limiting factor and the depth of investigation restricted by the electrical skin depth. Currently, these instruments seem to be ideally suited to rapid, large-scale, reconnaissance surveys for the detection of more deeply-lying archaeological or geomorphological features, but may yet challenge the quality of traditional earth resistance data for very near surface targets. Rough or uneven ground conditions can be problematic, causing poor coupling between the insulating electrodes and the subsurface.

1.7.2 Seismic methods
Seismic methods use low energy acoustic waves transmitted by vibration through the host medium and can be used effectively in both marine and terrestrial environments. Velocities of seismic waves vary from c 200 m/s in soil up to 7000 m/s in solid geological units and, at the frequencies deployed, can result in relatively long wavelengths, generally >1 m. This restricts the archaeological application of seismic methods to relatively large-scale features. For shallow, terrestrial, investigations the energy source can be as simple as a sledgehammer striking a flat metal plate in the ground, with the resulting vibrations measured by a line of regularly spaced geophone sensors. Each geophone is secured to the ground by a metal spike and consists of a suspended coil wound around a core of high magnetic permeability, in the field of a strong permanent magnet. Vibrations are then transferred through the spike to the coil to produce a proportional electric current. Multi-core cables are used to connect the entire array of geophones to a suitable multi-channel seismograph that amplifies the signals and records the time when the vibrations reach each geophone.

Energy from a seismic source travels as both a direct wave spreading out through the surface layer and also into successively deeper layers in the subsurface. On meeting an interface between two layers, part of the energy is reflected back to the surface and the remainder continues at a refracted angle. Assuming the lower layer has a higher velocity, an angle of *critical refraction* exists where the incident wave will travel parallel to the interface at this higher velocity, with some of its energy returning to the ground surface as an expanding head wave before the slower direct wave.

This difference in travel path forms the basis of the *seismic refraction* method, where the travel time of the refracted wave is measured from the first received energy for each geophone along the spread from the source, and subsequently used to estimate the depth to the subsurface interface. The seismic refraction method requires the velocity to increase with each subsequently deeper layer, a condition that may not always be met for typical archaeological surveys (Ovenden 1994), but has been successfully applied during the investigation of certain archaeological features, such as the *vallum* south of Hadrian's wall in Northumberland (Goulty *et al.* 1990).

An alternative approach is to use the *seismic reflection* technique that, analogous to GPR, records the amplitude variation of the received signal at each geophone over a suitable time window. For each source location seismic reflection data is often recorded at several locations that share a common mid-point (CMP) between the source and receiver. Multiple observations of buried reflectors are then recorded at successively later travel times and the data reduced to a single trace with a much improved signal-to-noise ratio. Field acquisition with this method is relatively slow compared to other near-surface techniques, but has been successfully applied in a number of archaeological surveys (e.g. Vafidis *et al.* 2003). The potential advantages of multi-fold CMP data acquisition have also been investigated for GPR survey (Booth *et al.* 2008; Pipan *et al.* 1999) together with the application of powerful seismic processing software, developed for oil exploration, which may equally be applied to GPR surveys over archaeological sites (e.g. Lehmann and Green 1999).

For shallow terrestrial imaging, seismic methods are disadvantaged by the need to use high-frequency acoustic sources, to create short wavelengths in the soil, while coupling the source energy effectively to the ground surface. The separation between the receiver geophones also needs to be reduced to obtain an appropriate sample interval, but this may be restricted where the amplitude of the source can potentially cause damage to the geophones. Attempts have been made to improve the applicability of acoustic techniques (e.g. Frazier *et al.* 2000; Hildebrand *et al.* 2002) – particularly using swept-frequency sources – that may well prove fruitful for imaging archaeological features buried under conditions unsuitable for other techniques, such as highly conductive alluvial soils (e.g. Metwaly *et al.* 2005).

1.7.3 Borehole methods
Many geophysical techniques are compromised by either the depth to the target archaeological features or, particularly on urban sites, the presence of considerably disturbed near-surface deposits (e.g. building rubble). One approach is to introduce the geophysical equipment into the ground through a borehole cored from the surface. This may, for example, take the form of a specially designed GPR transmitter that can be lowered down the borehole and measurements made to a receiver mounted on either the surface or in a second borehole. Equally, seismic sources and geophones, earth resistance electrodes or even magnetometers may be used for borehole investigations. Active source-receiver instruments (e.g. GPR) allow transmission tomography methods to be applied from deviations of the travel path as the transmitter and receiver are lowered down two separate boreholes.

The major disadvantage with these techniques is the necessity to introduce an invasive borehole into the site that may damage the buried archaeological remains. In some cases the information gained from a borehole geophysical survey may outweigh these concerns, particularly when boreholes have to be sunk for other invasive geotechnical investigations.

1.7.4 Micro gravity

Variations in the local acceleration of the Earth's gravitational field, caused by the contrast in density of the underlying structures, have been successfully used at an appropriate scale to investigate civil engineering or archaeological features (Arzi 1975; Di Filippo *et al.* 2000). By far the greatest success has been achieved using appropriate high-sensitivity gravimeters to locate air-filled void features, which, by definition, demonstrate a considerable density variation from the host structure (e.g. Blížkovsky 1979; Butler 1984; Fajklewicz 1976; Linford 1998; Linnington 1966).

In essence, a gravimeter consists of a spring-suspended weight and a means to record accurately any varying deflection in the presence of the local gravitational field. Practical instruments are highly sensitive and compensate both for changes in the ambient temperature and for vibrations at the sampling point. The resulting data must then be processed to account for a range of variables, including the diurnal variation of the Earth's gravitational field and even the micro-topography of the site under investigation and any large buildings nearby.

1.7.5 Radiometric methods

Radiation detectors can be used to determine the location and concentration of certain commercially viable radioactive ore bodies, such as uranium. While the attenuation of radioactive particles is relatively high in soil or rock, particularly for *alpha* and *beta* particles that will only travel short distances, *gamma* photons offer more promise (Ruffell and Wilson 1998). The most common sources of *gamma* radiation are the elements potassium, uranium and thorium that may be found in the constituent minerals forming many archaeological sites. Any contrast or greater concentration of these radioactive elements should, theoretically, be detectable with a scintillation counter of high enough sensitivity. For example, measurements of *gamma*-ray emissions within the walled Roman town at Silchester, Hampshire, U.K., revealed a much lower count rate from the flint and chalk building remains than the substantially higher background value caused by the presence of ^{40}K in the soil. Mapping the response with a towed scintillation counter demonstrated significant variations, possibly indicating both the location of building remains and the differing depth of soil cover across the site.

1.7.6 Thermal sensing

Variations in ground surface temperature can be influenced by the presence of buried archaeological features and are usually recorded by airborne infrared scanners that are able to cover large areas in a single swathe. Some attempts at ground-based thermal mapping have also been made (e.g. Clark 1996, Fig. 11), but these have been most successful for investigating historic building fabrics rather than for buried archaeological remains (e.g.

Brooke 1987; Kooiman and de Jongh 1994). Direct measurements of soil temperature with ground-contacting thermocouples have also been investigated, but the heat generated by friction when inserting the probe into the ground was found to slow data acquisition with this method of survey (Bellerby *et al.* 1990).

1.7.7 Self-potential
Electrolyte flow in ground water, and across any chemical potential gradient, can cause subtle variations in naturally occurring background potentials, for example across a gradient formed in a concentration of ferric and ferrous ions produced by localised burning of iron oxides in the soil. The application to archaeological prospecting was initially investigated by Wynn and Sherwood (1984) and is attractive for its relative simplicity and the low cost of the equipment required.

Field measurements are made between two non-polarising electrodes connected to a suitable high-impedance volt meter. However, care should be taken to account for the influence of topographic changes, buried metal (e.g. pipelines), stray currents from power sources, ground water movements and changes in temperature, as any of these factors will affect the local self-potential. Even the bioelectrical activity of large plants and trees is sufficient to create a detectable anomaly (Telford *et al.* 1976).

Drahor (2004) provides a summary of the possible sources of self-potential anomalies with regard to archaeological features and demonstrates the success of the technique for detecting burnt structures. However, the advantages of the low equipment costs for this method should be considered against the slow rate of acquisition and the difficulty in obtaining useable field data, and subsequently the often complex interpretation required. Burnt features are also readily detected by the more rapid magnetic techniques that should usually be considered in the first instance.

1.7.8 Induced polarisation
The effect of polarisation during the ionic conduction of an electrical current through the soil is a recognised constraint when using direct current for an earth resistance survey (see Section 1.3, Earth resistance survey). Electrode polarisation will also be influenced by subtle membrane polarisation effects associated with buried features and may be measured using a modified earth resistance array. Time-domain measurements are made by applying a square wave signal to the current electrodes, and then recording the decay of any induced polarisation voltage over a period of time shortly after the applied field has been removed. Higher-frequency alternating waveforms, generally between 0.0625 Hz and 1000 Hz, may also be used for measurements of phase shift in the frequency domain.

Aspinall and Lynam (1968) recognised the possible application of induced polarisation methods for archaeological survey, and subsequent field experiments demonstrated the potential for identifying a buried humus-filled ditch and bank that compared favourably with results from a simultaneous earth resistance survey (Aspinall and Lynam 1970, Fig. 57). A more recent application of this technique used frequency-domain measurements (also known as *spectral induced polarisation*) to locate a Bronze Age trackway, constructed from wooden planks, found in the Federsee bog near Lake Konstanz, Germany (Schleifer *et al.* 2002). The well preserved cell structure of the waterlogged wood exhibited a strong polarisation effect – producing a peak phase shift at a frequency of approximately 5 Hz – that located the feature.

1.7.9 Multi channel instruments and sensor platforms

The use of vehicle-towed sensor platforms, utilising differential GPS/GNSS, inertial systems and fluxgate compasses for navigational and positional information, has recently been explored and enables deployment of combination of multi-channel instruments for the rapid survey of large areas (Gaffney *et al.* 2012). For example, the University of Leicester has developed a system (*Figure 1*), configured with an array of caesium magnetometer and electromagnetic sensors. Results compare favourably with data collected with a hand-operated caesium magnetometer cart and were completed in a fraction of the time required for the more conventional survey (Leech and Hill 2008).

Towed multi-channel GPR antennas are also now available, offering the ability to capture very dense data-sets, equivalent to a traverse separation of approximately 0.1 m, from a 2 m wide instrument swathe (Trinks *et al.* 2010; Neubauer *et al.* 2012). While the initial cost of these systems is very high, the benefits of such instrumentation are clear when considering the very large-scale application of GPR survey (e.g. Neubauer *et al.* 2002).

Multichannel earth resistance instruments with different electrode separations (e.g. in the form of three different potential-measuring dipoles a as in the ARP©, *Figure 8d*) can acquire simultaneously data from different depths, and produce results that can be compared with multi-coil LFEM systems that record different depth channels simultaneously (e.g. DualEM 421S, *Figure 18*).

1.8 METAL DETECTING

Metal detectors are a special form of EM instruments (see Section 1.5, Low-frequency electromagnetic methods), but mention of them is separated out here because their applications are significantly different to other specialised EM techniques, and because their use solely to find and recover metal objects is contentious.

Depending on the instrumentation used, metal detectors emit a pulsed or continuous EM signal that generates detectable and characteristic eddy currents in targets of conducting metals. Depending on their sophistication, metal detectors can be sensitive to signals from small objects – such as individual coins at depths up to about 0.3 m – to larger items at greater depths. Detectors can usually be tuned to screen out unwanted responses and to discriminate in favour of certain metals.

Although initially mainly built for military use, development of these instruments has been driven in part by demand from hobbyists. However, these guidelines refer to the use of

metal detectors for archaeological field evaluation, rather than as a hobby. Nonetheless, all metal detector users are strongly advised to abide by their national guidelines or codes of practice. The 1992 Valetta Treaty specifically requires to obtain prior authorisation for their use, if such is foreseen by national legislation
(see Part II, 6.2).

If metal detector investigations are to be included in field evaluation they should be integrated with other relevant prospecting methods, as appropriate. Since metal detecting usually involves the recovery and removal of artefacts, it is imperative that this form of site evaluation is fully justified, is part of an agreed project design, and includes the use of appropriate field methodologies, subsequent conservation, reporting and deposition to an acceptable standard.

To be effective, a metal detector survey should use skilled operators with suitable instruments, working consistently and systematically (*Figure 22*). Recovered material should be located individually using GPS/GNSS or electronic measurements. Alternatively, a previously established grid with cells not larger than 10 m can be used to report finds within these units.

Archaeological artefacts must not be removed from the ground without recording the stratigraphy of the surrounding soil matrix in a systematic excavation. By contrast, metal detector surveys are only acceptable on the assumption that the artefacts recovered are no longer deposited in their original context and their shovel-extraction therefore does not destroy important

Figure 22: Systematic metal detector survey of an area that has been divided into grid cells.

archaeological stratigraphic information. It hence should normally only take place on land under arable conditions where the extraction does not disturb ground below the plough-zone. It may also be acceptable on sites under pasture, where there is unequivocal evidence that the area was subject to arable cultivation in recent years, provided that the extraction of material is restricted to the former modern plough-zone.

Metal detecting may in some circumstances be justified over areas that are destined for development and/or excavation, and that have been stripped of topsoil; in these cases controlled metal detecting can be an asset both during the excavation and in the recovery of artefacts from spoil.

1.9 GEOCHEMICAL METHODS

Geochemical methods (phosphate analysis, multi-element analysis and lipid analysis) are normally used to assist interpretation of other investigation techniques, whether on an intra-site or a landscape scale. Geochemical data on their own provide limited archaeological insight. A review of geochemical methods is provided by Heron (2001); see also English Heritage (2007).

2. ANALYSIS OF GEOPHYSICAL DATA

2.1 DATA TREATMENT

Once geophysical data have been collected it is necessary to process them for interpretation and presentation. The advent of powerful and affordable personal computing equipment has revolutionised this aspect of archaeological geophysics over the last fifteen years and several specialised software packages are now available. Detailed discussion of the reasons for and application of numerical processing algorithms can be found in a number of textbooks and software manuals (Gaffney and Gater 2003; Scollar *et al.* 1990; Walker 2005; Schmidt 2013a). Two guiding principles that underlie such discussions are important. Numerical processing can never be a substitute for poor raw data and the surveyor's aim should always be to collect the highest quality measurements in the field. Furthermore, every numerical modification of the original field data should be carried out for a clear purpose and no processing algorithm should be used blind without a full understanding of its implications.

The majority of numerical processing algorithms encountered in archaeological geophysical surveys fall into one of four categories (Schmidt 2013b; English Heritage 2008):

1. Those designed to mitigate for artefacts introduced into the data by the prospecting instrumentation, the operator or environmental conditions (data improvement).

2. Those that use the improved data and apply processing steps that are pertinent to the geophysical data collected with a specific technique, like spike removal, filtering, interpolation, or specialised processing like migration of GPR data and reduction-to-the-pole for magnetometer data (data processing).
3. Those that are applied to images created from the geophysical data and employ generic digital image processing methods to enhance certain features of interest (image processing). Since information content is already lost when converting the data into images these image processing techniques are not discussed here.
4. Those that use mathematical descriptions of the geophysical measurement process to model or infer information about causative features from the measured anomalies (inversion).

2.1.1 Data improvement: mitigating data collection artefacts

Magnetometer data

Scollar *et al.* (1990) and Aspinall *et al.* (2008) identify a number of sources of errors in magnetometer data resulting from field procedures. Computational procedures have been developed to detect and reduce the effects of many of these and maximise the clarity of archaeological anomalies present in the data-set. The most common corrections are discussed below and illustrated in *Figure 23* (alternate terms for a procedure are listed in parentheses after each heading).

Edge matching (equalising data grid shifts, micro-levelling)

A large survey will typically be composed of a mosaic of rectangular survey blocks or data grids surveyed at different times. One of the first procedures carried out after data collection is to combine these individual data grids into a single composite data-set. However, differences in temperature and other environmental conditions as well as recalibration of the magnetometer during the survey can result in data grids exhibiting different background measurement levels leading to visible discontinuities between the edges of adjacent data grids. Adjusting the mean or median of each data grid to a common value (often zero) by addition of a constant to each measurement value within the data grid is usually sufficient to eliminate edge discontinuities in magnetometer data (Eder-Hinterleitner *et al.* 1996). Only in extreme cases, such as the proximity of large modern ferrous structures, should more sophisticated methods, based upon analysis of the local statistics of measurements close to each data grid edge be required (e.g. Haigh 1992). Data improved in this way are often referred to as 'minimally processed' and images of these can usually be accepted in lieu of raw data. However, the raw measurement data prior to such treatment have always to be archived.

Spike removal (despiking)

Magnetometer sensor instability can occasionally cause isolated extreme readings, or spikes, in the survey data, and small pieces of highly magnetised iron lying on the ground surface can cause similar artefacts. Such distracting measurements may be distinguished by their large difference from neighbouring values within the data grid. Typically a thresholded median or mean filter is used to detect and replace such extreme values (Scollar *et al.* 1990). In order to identify such spikes even at the edges of data grids it

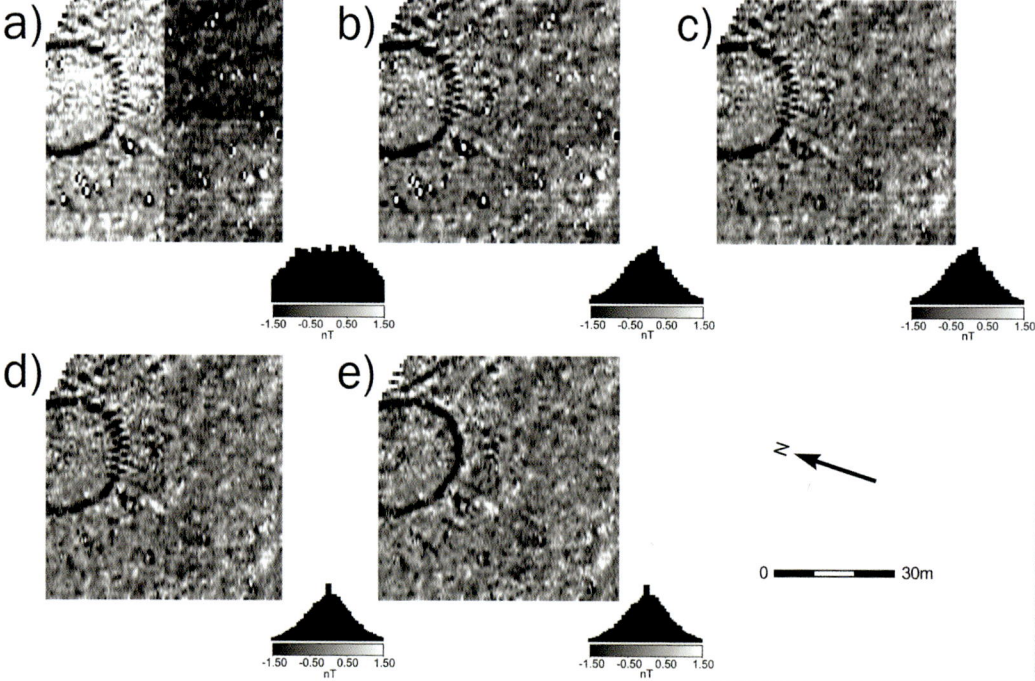

is often useful to improve and combine all data into a composite before applying spike removal. The technique is therefore sometimes classed as data processing and not data improvement. Methods that treat spikes as statistical outliers from the overall data distribution have also been developed and offer the advantage that they can be applied to randomly collected data before interpolation onto a regular grid (e.g. Ciminale and Loddo 2001).

Where spike removal has been used to suppress anomalies caused by surface iron objects, care should be taken with subsequent interpretation of the data. It is possible for the despiking operation to remove the high-magnitude positive peak of such small dipolar anomalies but leave the adjacent negative values, which are often of smaller absolute magnitude. Without the positive peak to provide context, these latter can be mistaken for negative archaeological anomalies. It must also be born in mind that spikes from ancient ferrous artefacts may be archaeologically significant (e.g. a distribution of Roman nails), and their removal is therefore not always desirable.

Figure 23: Common corrections for magnetometer data.
(a) composite plot of four data grids combined with no corrections; (b) the same four data grids combined, following edge matching, whereby discontinuities between data grids are reduced; (c) with additional spike removal where distracting dipolar responses are lessened; (d) after destriping, which had been most evident on the right half of the area; (e) after correcting line displacement errors with the most obvious effect on the circulinear anomaly, although other anomalies have also been clarified. This manipulation of the data is particularly clear in the positional adjustment of the incomplete lines in the top left corner.

Destriping

Magnetometer surveys collected in bi-directional (zigzag) mode can exhibit striping where successive traverses appear as alternating light and dark bands when the data are plotted. This is because magnetometers can exhibit directional sensitivity (sometimes called 'heading error'): a change in the value measured by the magnetometer depending on the direction it faces relative to magnetic north. In fluxgate gradiometers it is usually caused by slight differences in alignment between the two differential sensors, and optically pumped magnetometers exhibit an inherent directional sensitivity that can be minimised by careful sensor alignment.

The standard method of correction is to assume that the bias caused by this effect is constant over an entire traverse and to subtract a constant value from all readings on the traverse, such that their mean or median is set to zero or to a value common to all traverses (e.g. Ciminale and Loddo 2001). Such technique also simultaneously removes the long-term zero drift exhibited by most types of magnetometers, providing the time taken to complete each traverse is short relative to the rate of instrument drift. However, where traverses are long (approximately 100 m), more sophisticated linear regression techniques may be required instead (Tabbagh 2003).

When destriping, care should be taken that linear anomalies parallel to the traverse direction are not erroneously removed by the process, particularly when their length is close to or greater than the traverse length and their magnitude is similar to the biases caused by the directional sensitivity. Eder-Hinterleitner *et al.* (1996) describe a destriping method that can protect such parallel anomalies against erroneous removal, but only if they are wider than the survey traverse separation. Hence, every effort should be made to reduce instrument directional sensitivity in the field rather than relying on post-acquisition processing to remove severe striping.

Correcting line displacement errors (destaggering)

Magnetometers are often set to take readings at regular time intervals and the position along the traverse at which each reading was taken is calculated on the assumption that travel speed was constant. However, variations in traversal rate can occur (because the operator encounters a steep incline and has to slow down, for example) and this can result in the sensor not being at the correct position when a reading is taken. When traverses are walked in zigzag (bi-directional) fashion, deleterious effects can be pronounced with linear anomalies crossing the traverses having their peak positions displaced in opposite directions on alternate traverses, leading to a 'staggered' appearance in plots of the data. Often, shifting each traverse to maximise cross-correlation with the two neighbouring traverses will correct for the effect (e.g. Ciminale and Loddo 2001); however, where significant variations in pace occur during a single traverse, re-interpolation of the sample interval may also be necessary (Eder-Hinterleitner *et al.* 1996). Such methods can only estimate the displacement that has occurred by making assumptions about how anomalies appearing on adjacent traverses should match up. Particular care should be taken to ensure that linear anomalies running diagonally to the traverse direction are not altered so that they appear perpendicular to the traverses after this operation. Thus, diligent field procedure should always be employed to minimise the need for post-acquisition correction of line displacement errors.

Earth resistance data
Scollar *et al.* (1990) and Schmidt (2013a) outline the problems that can occur with earth resistance measurements. The majority are best avoided by careful attention during data collection. However, two types of error are often impossible to eliminate completely and are susceptible to mitigation by numerical procedures.

Edge matching (equalising data grid shifts, micro-levelling)
Weather conditions may change during the course of a large earth resistance survey, causing changes in the soil moisture content. Such changes will influence the average resistivity of the sub-surface and it is possible that adjacent data grids measured on different days will exhibit a discontinuity along their common edge. Where changes in soil moisture conditions have been relatively minor, corrective procedures similar to those used for magnetometer surveys usually suffice. However, more severe variations in conditions may require more complex pre-treatment to individual data grids such as re-scaling the data range (Schmidt 2013a) or the removal of a first order trend. In extreme cases it may not be possible to entirely remove edge discontinuities caused by changes in field conditions.

Spike removal (despiking)
Surface conditions such as concentrations of stones or uneven topography may result in poor electrical contact between the ground and one or more of the earth resistance electrodes. This can result in anomalously high or low resistance values being measured. As such measurements will exhibit large differences from neighbouring values it is possible to detect and remove them using the same types of procedures used to remove spikes in magnetometer surveys (as with magnetometer surveys, this can be considered to be data processing, not data improvement). However, if there are large numbers of such measurements with high contact resistance it may be advisable to re-measure the data in the field because their post-acquisition removal reduces the number of truly independent measurements in the resulting data-set.

Ground penetrating radar data
The level of post-acquisition processing required for GPR data will depend, in part, on the specific aims of the survey (e.g. for the production of individual profiles or multiple traverse data-sets, or for display as time or depth slices) and, perhaps to a lesser extent, the type of radar equipment in use. Useful summaries of appropriate GPR data processing techniques can be found in Annan (2004) and Daniels (2004), and more specific archaeological applications are considered in Conyers and Goodman (1997), Leckebusch (2003) and Conyers (2012).

As with other geophysical methods good field technique will minimise many data acquisition artefacts and particular care should be taken to maintain good antenna coupling with the ground surface. The GPR data processing procedures discussed below represent general considerations arising under typical field conditions and should be read in conjunction with Sections 1.4 and 2.1.3.

Individual trace repositioning and interpolation (rubber-banding)
The majority of GPR data will be collected at a high density along survey lines using either a system triggered by a distance measuring odometer wheel or continuous time-based trace acquisition with additional positional information. This positional information may be provided through the manual insertion of fiducial markers as the antenna passes distance markers along the survey guide rope or, for more recent instruments, simultaneous GPS/GNSS measurements or autotracking Total Station information. Regardless of the system in use it is often necessary to reposition and interpolate the raw GPR traces to account for slight variations in the collected sample density because of changes in the speed of acquisition for continuously triggered systems, odometer wheel slippage or calibration error, or the lower density of GPS/GNSS or fiducial data compared to the rate of GPR capture. Despite the inherent errors associated with all (semi-)automated methods of positional control, adequately processed data-sets contain few, if any, positional artefacts.

Zero offset removal (DC shift or dewow)
This process corrects the mean value of each trace to a near zero value to account for any DC offset that may have been introduced by the sampling electronics during the period of data acquisition. Slow time variations of such offset (e.g. one cycle per trace) may also be removed and are referred to as 'dewow'.

Time zero alignment
Some temporal down-trace variation of the first recorded signal ('time zero') on each trace may occur from electronic drift across a data-set. This drift can be corrected by aligning the common direct-wave response present in every trace, often through picking and adjusting to a single minimum amplitude threshold (e.g. Conyers 2004). However, such processing is rarely necessary for modern systems that are equipped with very stable time control.

Time varying signal gain
An appropriate gain can be applied to amplify lower amplitude, later reflections caused both by the attenuation of the signal in the propagation medium and by the spreading loss of the expanding radar wave front with depth (e.g. Jol and Bristow 2003).

For this an appropriate down-trace time window can be chosen, which may include the air-wave response to improve resolution of very near-surface non-planar reflections; but care should be taken to avoid the suppression of significant horizontal reflectors, if present (e.g. Conyers 2004, Fig. 6.3). Using averaged survey transects an 'autogain' can be calculated that is the applied to all traces.

PART IV: INTRODUCTION TO ARCHAEOLOGICAL GEOPHYSICS

Frequency filtering
Both low-frequency energy, associated with antenna-to-ground interactions, and high-frequency noise can be suppressed by the application of suitable frequency filters, generally matched to the frequency range of the specific antenna in use.

2.1.2 Data processing
In some situations filtering methods can be employed to accentuate anomalies of interest within the survey data while suppressing the effects of those considered less

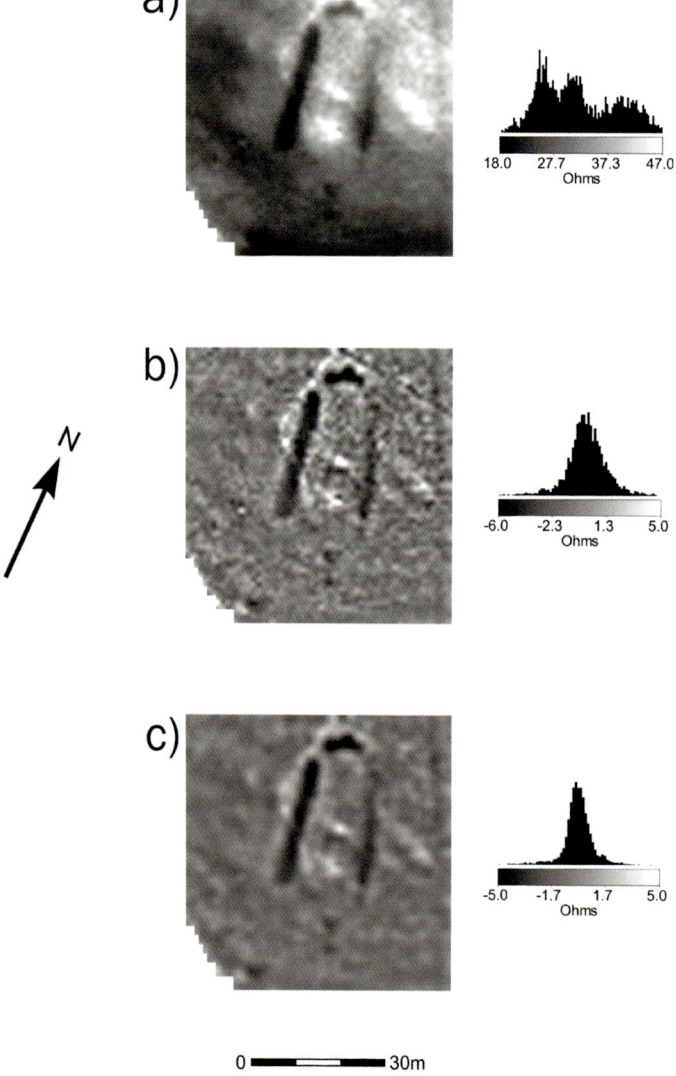

Figure 24: Earth resistance data over a long barrow. The long barrow's U-shaped ditch is defined by low resistance (black) over a variable background response, showing the effect of high-pass and low-pass filtering: (a) raw data showing variable background resistance across the surveyed area; (b) removal of variable background using a 3 m radius Gaussian high-pass filter; (c) main archaeological responses in the data further emphasised by smoothing with a 1 m radius Gaussian low-pass filter.

archaeologically relevant. A wide variety of such algorithms exists, many of which were not originally developed for geophysical data-sets and Scollar *et al.* (1990) review a number of those most relevant to archaeological geophysics. Perhaps the most commonly applied are convolution operators that calculate a weighted local average around each data value then either deduct it from or substitute it for the original value (often termed high- and low-pass filtering, respectively). Low-pass filtering can be used to suppress the effects of uncorrelated measurement noise between adjacent readings while high-pass filtering can remove the effects of large-scale geological trends within the data allowing archaeological anomalies to be discerned more clearly (*Figure 24*).

Filtering is usually unnecessary for magnetic gradiometer data, but it should be considered for earth resistance data where archaeological anomalies are often superimposed upon larger-scale trends caused by geological and hydrological changes. Where such techniques have been applied it is essential that they are identified and explained. Reference to standard texts on the subject is acceptable, although the choice of any variable parameters should be detailed. All such algorithms accentuate some aspects of the data at the expense of suppressing others, and many have the potential to produce spurious processing artefacts, which may then be misinterpreted by either the contractor or the client. To guard against this eventuality the survey report should explain why a particular series of processes was necessary, summarising the benefits to interpretation. It is misleading to conceal the poor quality of the original data by applying merely cosmetic enhancements.

2.1.3 Modelling and inversion
Data modelling considers idealised forms of the types of buried archaeological feature that might be detected in a geophysical survey and, by describing mathematically the physical processes by which such features influence surface geophysical measurements, predicts the form of geophysical anomaly that should result. By comparing a set of synthetic anomalies with those detected in real survey data it is sometimes possible to estimate parameters such as the shape and burial depth of archaeological features. By contrast, data inversion attempts to predict causative archaeological features directly from the survey data by applying the mathematical inverse of the operators used for synthetic modelling to the field measurements.

Such techniques are usually not necessary for standard archaeological area surveys where the layout of archaeological features can be determined from a plan view of the geophysical anomalies. However, the anomalies generated by vertical electrical sections are often complex and the shapes and burial depths of causative features cannot always be directly inferred from the geophysical measurements. For this type of data, numerical inversion techniques may be applied to clarify the vertical definition of buried archaeological structures (Papadopoulos *et al.* 2007; Drahor *et al.* 2008).

The process often proceeds iteratively, first inverting the data, then modelling the measurements that would be expected, given the inferred features, and then using a comparison between the modelled and real data to improve the inversion. This process is

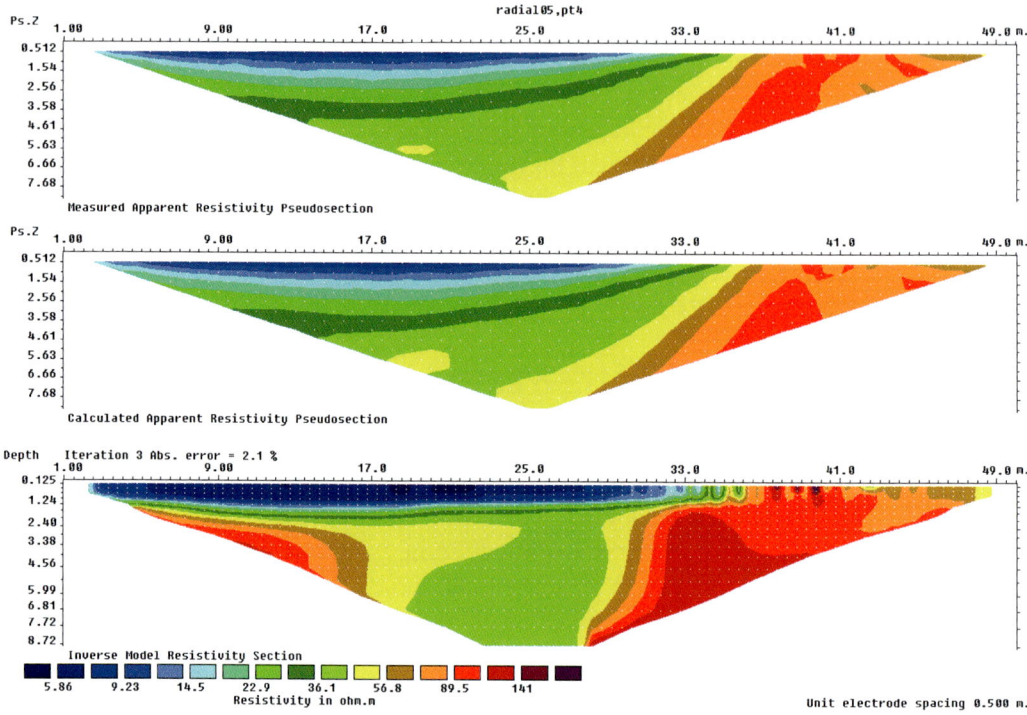

repeated until the modelled measurements match the real measurements to an acceptable degree (*Figure 25*; Loke and Barker 1996).

While not generally required for standard archaeological surveys where the objective is to identify the presence of archaeological features, modelling techniques can also be applied to magnetic data to estimate characteristics of the causative archaeological features. As magnetic anomalies cannot be uniquely attributed to one particular causative feature (Blakely 1996), it is usually not possible to apply inversion methods such as those used for electrical sections. However, by making a number of reasonable simplifying assumptions it is possible to model the geometry of the buried features likely to have caused a particular detected anomaly (e.g. Eppelbaum *et al.* 2001; Neubauer and Eder-Hinterleitner 1998).

Forward modelling of GPR data is both complicated and computationally intensive compared to the inversion of earth resistance or magnetic data (e.g. Conyers and Goodman 1997, plate 2a; Daniels 2004, 37–67, C3).

Figure 25: Inversion of an electrical section over a ditch. The data shows a low resistance (dark blue) anomaly. The top picture shows the pseudosection created from the raw electrical measurements, while the bottom picture shows the best-fitting subsurface model calculated by inversion of these measurements. The middle picture shows the estimated pseudosection that would have been measured for the modelled subsurface.

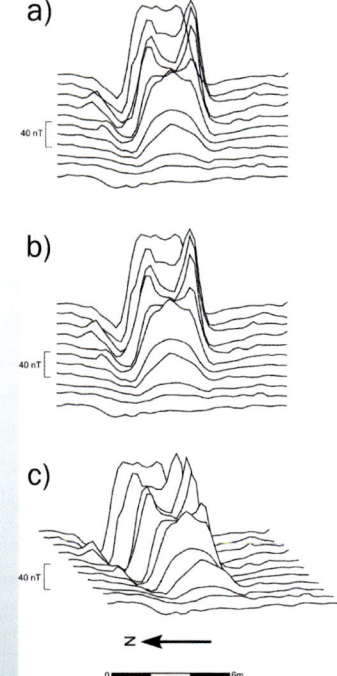

Figure 26: Different trace plot displays.
(a) Basic trace plot of a magnetometer survey over a kiln feature; (b) the same trace plot with hidden lines removed to give an impression of a surface; (c) plotted with successive traverses increasingly offset to the side to create a three-dimensional effect.

However, attempts are often made to reduce the complex transmitted signal, or wavelet, produced by a GPR to an ideal impulse response function through wavelet optimisation or deconvolution techniques. This process is often complicated further by the time variant attenuation of the incident wavelet as it passes through the subsurface, but deconvolution can often prove effective for the suppression of certain repetitive down-trace signal artefacts such as antenna 'ringing' over near-surface conductive objects (e.g. Conyers 2004).

In addition, the use of wave-front migration techniques to collapse the hyperbolic response from point-reflectors – caused by the progressively spreading pattern of radar energy through the ground – is sometimes considered to be a form of data modelling (e.g. Conyers 2004; Linford 2006). However, migrated GPR data-sets are rarely, if ever, confirmed by the application of a suitable forward model and subsequent comparison against the original data. Migration can often aid the resolution of detailed structures within complex anomalies caused by the overlapping response of many individual point-source targets, but may not be beneficial to every data-set.

2.2 DATA DISPLAY

Graphical presentation of geophysical survey data is an essential step in visualising, understanding and interpreting the results. Appropriate data plots should be provided in the survey report to support the interpretations made by the practitioner and to help both specialist and non-specialist readers to follow the reasoning set out in the report text. A number of different display formats have been developed for geophysical data and the benefits and limitations of each are summarised below. For most survey reports, greyscale plots are the primary presentation format, supported by some of the plot types discussed below where these aid the interpretation.

2.2.1 Trace plots (X-Y traces, stacked traces)

Before the development of portable digital computers, trace plots were a common method for displaying magnetometer surveys, as the analogue output from a magnetometer could be directly connected to an X-Y chart recorder, which displayed the data as they were collected (Clark and Haddon-Reece 1972–3). Each instrument traverse is depicted as an approximately horizontal line but the line trace deviates above or below a base (zero) level in proportion to the magnitude of the magnetometer measurement at that position (*Figure 26*). Subsequent traverses are plotted parallel to the first, offset at increasing distances up or down the page.

In its simplest implementation the trace plot has only one variable plotting parameter – the vertical scale – which specifies how far the trace should swing above or below the base level in response to a unit change in measurement. Thus the trace plot has a relatively low degree of operator subjectivity and anomalies of widely varying magnitudes can all be discerned on the same plot. Additionally, unlike other common techniques which display the data in plan, the trace plot depicts vertical profiles across anomalies, which makes the distinctive signatures of some types of anomalies readily apparent (such as the distinctive kiln anomaly in *Figure 26*). Hence, they provide a useful initial impression of the relative overall variation in magnitude of anomalies in an unprocessed data-set and, particularly when used to plot small areas extracted from the overall survey, can greatly aid interpretation of specific anomalies. However, for the trace plot to be useful, it is essential that a graphical indication be provided showing the vertical scale used to represent variations in the measured values.

A drawback of the profile view is that an excessive number of extreme measurements (especially spikes) in the data-set can render the plot visually unintelligible. In this case it is necessary to truncate (or clip) such values before display. The very large magnetometer surveys that are now practical with modern multi-sensor instruments can also cause problems as the sheer number of traverses needing to be displayed means that there is not enough space in the plotting area to distinguish one from the next. Thus, it is now not always practical for a survey report to provide a trace plot of the unprocessed survey data in its entirety, although plots of sub-areas containing distinctive anomalies can still be advantageously employed to support interpretations.

Elaborations to the basic trace plot have been introduced to create a more solid three-dimensional appearance. Traverses plotted near the bottom of the plot are considered to be closer to the viewer than those farther up, and a straightforward method to give a visual impression of depth is to hide line segments in the background that would be obscured by anomalies rising up in the foreground (hidden line removal) (*Figure 26b*). The impression can be strengthened by laterally offsetting traverses in proportion to their distance from the viewer to provide a pseudo-isometric view (*Figure 26c*).

2.2.2 Contour plots
Contour plots display the survey data in plan using a series of contour lines (or isopleths) to show the positions where the magnitudes of the geophysical quantity being measured (e.g. magnetometer readings) crosses one of a predetermined set of threshold values (*Figure 27*) (Davis and Sampson 1986, chapter 5). If the survey data contain mainly localised variations from a base level that is relatively constant over the whole area, it is

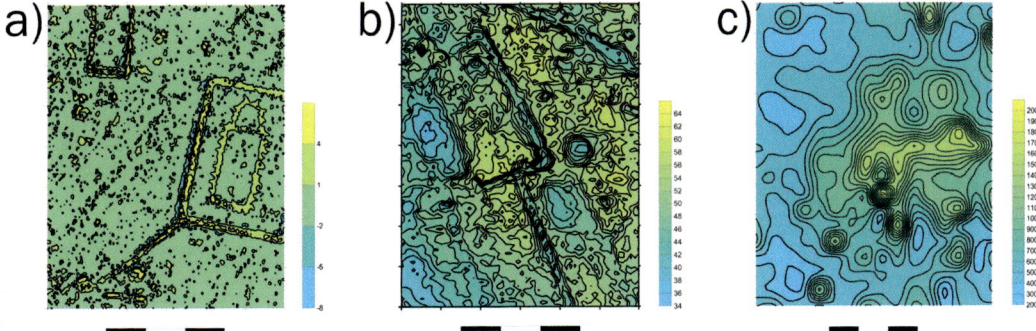

Figure 27: Colour contour plots.
(a) Magnetometer data where the 1 nT and 4 nT contours outline the linear footings of timber buildings and adjacent enclosure ditches; (b) earth resistance data with a varying regional background where the choice of contouring has been less successful at isolating the anomalies; (c) smoothly varying magnetic susceptibility data with elevated readings coinciding with the location of a Roman villa and lower values associated with an adjacent river floodplain.

possible to produce an effective contour plot that outlines the important archaeological anomalies (*Figure 27a*). However, the choice of the particular data thresholds to contour is critical, so contour plotting involves a high degree of subjectivity. Where the background data level varies across the plotting area, many different contour values are needed to emphasise localised details against all the different base levels. Furthermore, whatever algorithm is used to create continuous contours from the data, the process intrinsically involves a degree of low-pass filtering, which will tend to smooth out the smaller-scale anomalies that are typically of great interest in archaeological surveys.

The net result of trying to select enough contours to counteract these problems can be a very 'busy', visually unintelligible, plot (see for example *Figure 27b*; and Scollar *et al.* 1990, Fig. 8.35). Hence, contour plots tend not to be suitable for depicting detailed area surveys containing complex archaeological anomalies. However, for low-resolution data-sets where the measured geophysical property varies smoothly across the survey area (*Figure 27c*), or to emphasis the large scale regional trends in a more densely sampled survey, contour plots can still be an effective means of presentation. They can also be deployed advantageously to highlight very high magnitude thermoremanent anomalies in magnetometer surveys. Wherever contour plots are used, it is essential that the contour values are labelled, as otherwise it is impossible to determine which are the peaks (highest values) and which the troughs (lowest values) in the plot.

2.2.3 Dot density plots

Dot density plots (*Figure 28a*) also plot the survey area in plan and were a popular means of displaying data-sets prior to the advent of affordable high-resolution computer graphics when computer monitors were monochrome and printers did not have high resolution half-tone or colour printing capabilities. The plotting area is divided into small sub-rectangles each corresponding to the footprint of one geophysical measurement. Black dots are placed randomly within each sub-rectangle with the total number assigned being determined according to the magnitude of the geophysical measurement at that point. The effect approximates to that of a printed greyscale plot, albeit one in which the half tone is readily visible. Dot density plots share many of the advantages of greyscale plots outlined below. However, the random assignment of dots means that the same plot, using the same plotting parameters, can appear different each time it is generated, possibly affecting which anomalies are highlighted or suppressed. Also, the need to sub-divide the plotting area into relatively large sub-rectangles, coupled with the fact that randomly placed dots do not create the same visual effect as a continuous periodic half-tone pattern, can emphasise discontinuities between adjacent measurements and lead to a blocky appearance.

2.2.4 Greyscale plots (greytone plots)

Greyscale plots (*Figure 28b–d*) are now the most commonly used and versatile method of displaying geophysical data in plan. As with dot density plots the survey area is divided into sub-rectangles each corresponding to the footprint of one field measurement, but in this case the rectangles are filled with a shade of grey related to the magnitude of the geophysical reading at that point. With modern computer graphics capabilities a large palette of grey shades can be used (typically between 100 and 256), providing a continuous variation in tone between white and black. This continuous gradation suppresses the perception of discontinuities between adjacent measurements, allowing the eye to concentrate on trends across the survey area; and the effect can be strengthened by interpolating the data to a higher resolution, so that each shaded sub-rectangle corresponds to one pixel on the display device being used.

Figure 28 (opposite page): Different display options for magnetometer data. (a) Dot density plot; (b) linear greyscale or half-tone plot (no interpolation); (c) linear greyscale plot of interpolated data; (d) equal area greyscale plot; (e) plot produced using a colour palette.

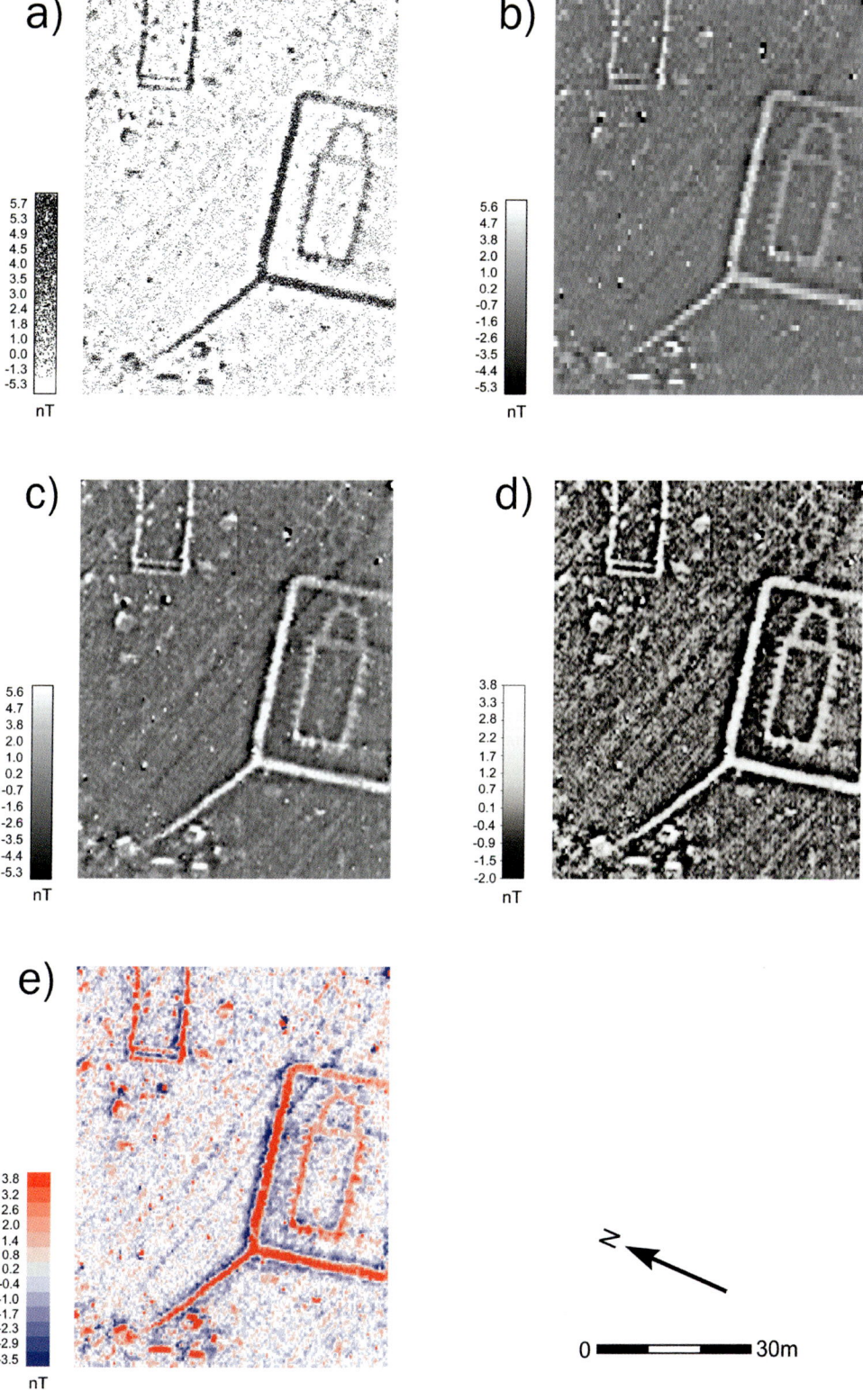

The greyscale can be assigned with white representing the lowest measured values, progressively darker shades of grey corresponding to higher values and black representing the highest values of all; or the assignment can be reversed, with black used for the lowest values and white for the highest (practitioners familiar with dot density plots often favour the former while those from an image processing background may prefer the latter). Furthermore, the thresholds between the measured values shaded with different levels of grey can be assigned in different ways, the most common choice being a linear mapping from the range of survey data values, although log-linear and equal-area (or histogram-equalised) assignments are also useful, depending on the statistical characteristics of the data being plotted. From the foregoing it should be clear that it is mandatory for every greyscale plot be accompanied by an assignment key (range-bar, annotated with values and units) to show how the measured values map to the shades of grey in the plot.

Greyscale plots of archaeological geophysical data often look similar to vertical black and white air photographs, a form of presentation readily familiar even to those with no experience of geophysical data interpretation. A variant of the basic plot, the shadow plot, strengthens this effect by pre-processing the survey data to accentuate edges and sharp gradients running in a pre-selected direction. The effect is similar to an air photograph of earthworks taken in strong oblique sunlight and can be effective in emphasising linear anomalies sharing a common alignment. A second variation is to replace the greyscale with a palette of different colours to produce a false-colour plot (*Figure 28e*), similar to the way that differing land surface elevations are colour coded in an atlas. However, it should be noted that the eye will tend to be drawn to the interfaces between contrasting colours, so that the overall visual effect will be that of a coloured contour plot. As with contour plots, careful choice of the colour thresholds can produce results that dramatically emphasise particular anomalies while other details are suppressed in the process. It is thus strongly recommended that where colour plots are used, a greyscale plot of the same data is also shown. In addition it has to be borne in mind that colour plots are sometimes reproduced in black-and-white, thereby losing their meaning; in the process colours with similar saturation may be assigned to the same greyscale (e.g. mid-red and mid-green show both as mid-grey). Consideration should also be made of people with differing colour-vision; 'safe' palettes can be found on the web.

2.2.5 Three-dimensional views
The isometric trace plots mentioned above can incorporate diminution towards a horizon point to provide perspective and enhance their three-dimensional impression. Introduction of a second set of parallel lines orthogonal to the instrument traverses then creates a wire-frame surface plot (*Figure 29a*) and the quadrilaterals so formed can be coloured and shaded (*Figure 29b*) to render the data as a solid three-dimensional surface (see for example Foley *et al.* 1991, chapter 15). An extension to this type of surface plot is the 'drape', where the shape of the plotted surface is determined by the actual topography of the area surveyed, whereas its colour is determined by the geophysical measurements – effectively a greyscale or false-colour plot is draped over the surface topography of the site (*Figure 29c*). Where the plotted surface represents site topography, exaggeration of the scale

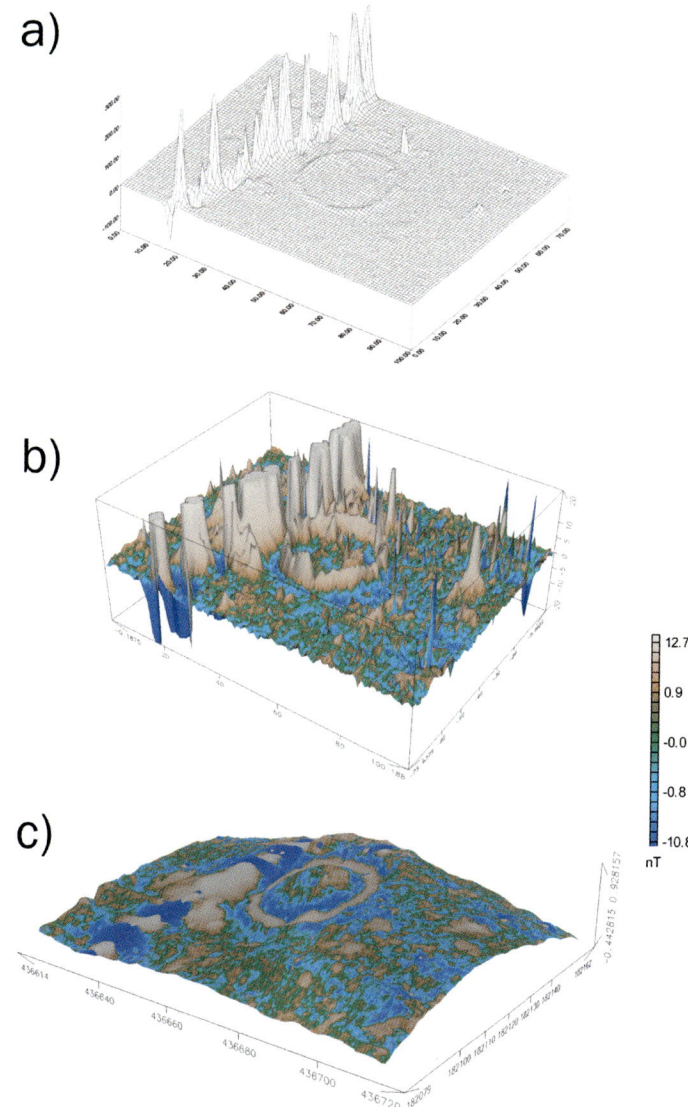

Figure 29: Three-dimensional representations of geophysical data.
(a) A wire-frame plot (with vertical scale exaggerated);
(b) a shaded surface plot (with vertical values truncated to ±20 nT); (c) a plot of the data draped over a digital terrain model (with vertical scale exaggerated).

of the vertical axis is often an effective way to highlight subtle changes in elevation. In this case it is important that the plot key makes clear the factor by which the vertical axis has been scaled relative to the two horizontal axes, in addition to the usual requirement for a grey/colour scale assignment key.

A different type of three-dimensional view can be used where a 3D volume of data has been imaged (as is often measured with GPR or electrical resistivity imaging (ERI) equipment). The resulting data can be displayed as either a false-perspective cut-away model or as an iso-surface where a threshold value is chosen and all parts of the volume where the geophysical value is below this threshold are considered transparent, while those parts above the threshold are rendered opaque (see *Figure 16d*). Iso-surface plots can assist in elucidating spatial relationships between anomalies associated with individual causative features, although the selection of an appropriate threshold level requires careful judgement.

All types of three-dimensional rendering can provide visually striking representations of the survey data but it should be borne in mind that they will emphasise anomalies in the foreground of the view while obscuring those further back. Thus the choice of viewpoint when creating the plot will determine which details are visible, and it should be recognised that plots from more than one different viewpoint may be necessary to display adequately all parts of the survey area.

Where a computer display screen is being used rather than a hard copy, it is possible to interactively change the viewpoint or animate a sequence of views as a 'fly-through' to overcome this difficulty, although it is not possible to reproduce this type of interactive presentation in the printed report – which currently is the authoritative reference for the survey project. Hence, while three-dimensional views can be used to good effect to highlight specific details within a geophysical data-set, they should not be the only type of graphical plot presented, but should be supported by more traditional plan representations, such as greyscale plots.

2.3 DATA INTERPRETATION

Raw geophysical data can be obtained, processed and presented, one way or another, by following instruction manuals and guidelines. However, the interpretation that follows generally requires a wider experience – encompassing an understanding of the site conditions and their history, the principles of archaeological geophysics, as well as the foibles of instruments and survey methodologies. A good knowledge of archaeology is of course important, as well as of geology and geomorphology. Ideally an interpreter will already have such experience, and will preferably have conducted and/or directed the fieldwork concerned personally (although it need not follow that the fieldworker is thereby automatically qualified in the subsequent interpretation of the data).

The factors that require consideration in arriving at an interpretation will vary from site to site, but should normally include at least the factors listed in Table 4. Any interpretation will normally take into account each of these factors, the emphasis varying according to circumstance, and should include consultation with colleagues and other relevant specialists where necessary. For instance, experience shows that where there is even the most meagre earthwork survival, the combination of topographical field survey and geophysical survey is highly beneficial to their joint interpretation. The degree of usefulness of the former will increase according to the condition of the earthworks and the intensity of the field survey. Likewise, where earthworks have been completely

Table 4: Factors that may affect the data.

Natural	Artificial
solid geology	landscape history
drift geology	known/inferred archaeological features
soil type	agricultural practices
soil magnetic susceptibility	modern interference
geomorphology	survey methodology
Surface conditions	data treatment
topography	any other available data
seasonality and weather history	

ploughed out, comparison with aerial photographic analysis and evidence from historic maps will also yield useful interpretative data.

Arriving at an interpretation that takes into account so many factors can be a finely balanced process and the outcome will be coloured by, and depend significantly upon, the experience of the interpreter. Above all it is crucial that any interpretation draws a clear line for the reader between demonstrable fact that is securely supported by the data, and less secure inference. Most importantly, it must be expressed clearly how the interpretation was arrived at, and the division between objective reasoning and more subjective circumstantial inference has to be made clear. The interpretation of archaeological geophysical data inevitably includes surmise – and this should be encouraged – but there should be no doubt precisely where the areas of uncertainty lie. Confidence in the interpretation of geophysical survey data can only come from transparency of the reasoning that links data acquisition to processing and interpretation. This is the foundation of scientific endeavour.

Here, we would only warn against a tendency to see and attribute significance to every detail – in other words, to over-interpret. Minutely annotated plots with laborious textual referencing of every apparently significant anomaly stretch the credibility and wear down the patience of readers. Generally speaking, it is preferable to exercise as much objectivity and restraint as possible, and to err towards less interpretation, resisting the embellishment of plots with wishful patterns and details.

While much importance is given to the graphical presentation of results (see Part II, 3.11), and it is often this, not the text, that holds the client's attention, it is important that the graphics are supported and complemented by precise written discussion as well. Especially if the interpreted features are attributed to particular classes, the scheme in use should be clearly laid out with a list of criteria for each attribution, possibly explained in detail in an appendix. For example, if a simple scheme is used that only distinguishes between possible archaeological features and anomalies of likely modern origin, criteria for this differentiation need to be laid out. Similarly, if a sophisticated scheme of archaeological feature interpretation is used the criteria need to be presented in detail (e.g. Gaffney *et al.* 2000, Table 1). Sometimes percentage 'confidence ratings' are assigned to the interpretation of geophysical anomalies (e.g. '40% likely to be of archaeological origin'). Although such judgement is inherently subjective, and likely to be different for different sites, attempts should be made to provide guidance as to the statements made, for example in an appendix.

Refinement of the interpretation of geophysical surveys is, to a significant degree, dependent upon the feedback of 'ground-truth' following the survey fieldwork, if possible from areas where geophysical anomalies were detected. Wherever possible every effort should be made to encourage such feedback and its subsequent dissemination into the general pool of accumulated experience (see Part II, 4). To aid this process, curators can stipulate that trial trenching and excavation reports are copied to the geophysical contractor, that mitigation and publication briefs make allowance for the results of geophysical surveys, and that reporting includes the post-excavation comments of the geophysical contractor (if appropriate).

Geophysical data cannot be used as 'negative evidence', since the lack of geophysical anomalies cannot be taken to imply a lack of archaeological features. However, where a corpus of previous work is available for the same environmental and geological conditions a statistical probability for the existence of archaeological features may be derived from the geophysical data, taking the resolving power of the used methodology into account. Such estimates have to be fully qualified and explained.

PART V: REFERENCES

ACAO 1993 *Model Briefs and Specifications for Archaeological Assessments and Field Evaluations*. Association of County Archaeological Officers

Annan, A P 2004 *Ground Penetrating Radar Principles, Procedures and Applications*. Ontario: Sensors and Software

Annan, A P and Cosway, S W 1992 'Simplified GPR beam model for survey design', *in* Society of Exploration Geophysicists, 62nd Annual Meeting 1992, New Orleans: Society of Exploration Geophysicists, 356–9

Arzi, A A 1975 'Microgravimetry for engineering applications'. *Geophys Prospecting* **23**, 408–25

Aspinall, A and Crummett, J G 1997 'The electrical pseudosection'. *Archaeol Prospection* **4**, 37–47

Aspinall, A, Gaffney, C F and Schmidt, A 2008 *Magnetometry for Archaeologists, Geophysical methods for archaeology*, Lanham: AltaMira Press.

Aspinall, A and Lynam, J T 1968 'Induced polarization as a technique for archaeological surveying'. *Prospezioni Archeol* **3**, 91–3

Aspinall, A and Lynam, J T 1970 'An induced polarisation instrument for the detection of near-surface features'. *Prospezioni Archeol* **5**, 67–75

Aspinall, A and Saunders, M K 2005 'Experiments with the square array'. *Archaeol Prospection* **12**, 115–29

Athanasiou, E N, Tsourlos, P I, Vargemezis, G N, Papazachos, C B and Tsokas, G N 2007 'Non-destructive DC resistivity surveying using flat-base electrodes'. *Near Surface Geophysics* **5**, 263–74

Bates, M R and Bates, C R 2000 'Multidisciplinary approaches to the geoarchaeological evaluation of deeply stratified sedimentary sequences: examples from Pleistocene and Holocene deposits in southern England, United Kingdom'. *J Archaeol Sci* **27**, 845–58

Bates, M R, Bates, C R and Whittaker, J E 2007 'Mixed method approaches to the investigation and mapping of buried Quaternary deposits: examples from southern England'. *Archaeol Prospection* **14**, 104–29

Bayley, J, Dungworth, D and Paynter, S 2001 *Archaeometallurgy*. Centre for Archaeology Guidelines **2001/01**. London: English Heritage

Becker, H 1995 'From nanotesla to picotesla, a new window for magnetic prospecting in archaeology'. *Archaeol Prospection* **2**, 217–28

Bellerby, T J, Noel, M J and Brannigan, K 1990 'A thermal method for archaeological prospection: preliminary investigations'. *Archaeometry* 32, 191–203

Bendjoudi, H, Weng, P, Guérin, R and Pastre, J F 2002 'Riparian wetlands of the middle reach of the Seine river (France): historical development, investigation and present hydrologic functioning. A case study', *Journal of Hydrology,* **263**(1–4), 131-155.

Bettess, F 1992 *Surveying for Archaeologists (rev edn)*. Durham: University of Durham

Bevan, B 1991 'The search for graves'. *Geophysics* **56**, 1310–19

Blakely, R J 1996 *Potential Theory in Gravity and Magnetic Applications*. Cambridge: Cambridge University Press

Blížkovsky, M 1979 'Processing and applications in microgravity surveys'. *Geophys Prospecting* **27**, 848–51

Booth, A D, Linford, N T, Clark, R A and Murray, T 2008 'Three-dimensional, multi-offset ground-penetrating radar imaging of archaeological targets', *Archaeological Prospection,* **15**(2), 93–112

Bowden, M (ed.) 1999 *Unravelling the Landscape: An Inquisitive Approach to Archaeology.* Stroud: Tempus

Breiner, S 1999 *Applications Manual for Portable Magnetometers.* San Jose: Geometrics

Brooke, C J 1987 'Ground-based remote sensing for archaeological information recovery in historic buildings'. *Internat J Remote Sensing* **8**, 1039–48

Brown, D H 2007 *Archaeological Archives: A Guide to Best Practice in Creation, Compilation, Transfer and Curation.* Birmingham: IfA on behalf of the Archaeological Archives Forum

Bruckner, H, Mullenhoff, M, Gehrels, R, Herda, A, Knipping, M and Vott, A 2006 'From archipelago to floodplain - geographical and ecological changes in Miletus and its environs during the past six millennia (Western Anatolia, Turkey)' *in* Eitel, B. (ed.) *Holocene Landscape Development and Geoarchaeological Research,* Stuttgart: Gebruder Borntraeger, 63–83

Butler, D K 1984 'Microgravimetric and gravity gradient techniques for detection of subsurface cavities'. *Geophysics* **49**, 1084–96

Campana, S and Dabas, M 2011 'Archaeological Impact Assessment: The BREBEMI Project (Italy)', *Archaeological Prospection,* **18**(2), 139–148

Canti, M G and Meddens, F M 1998 'Mechanical coring as an aid to archaeological projects'. *J Field Archaeol* **25**, 97–105

Carey, C J, Brown, T G, Challis, K C, Howard, A J and Cooper, L 2006 'Predictive modelling of multiperiod geoarcheological resources at a river confluence: a case study from the Trent-Soar, UK'. *Archaeol Prospection* **13**, 241–50

Castaldini, D, Cardarelli, A, Cattani, M, Panizza, M and Piacentini, D 2007 'Geo-archaeological aspects of the Modena plain (Northern Italy)', *Physio-Géo,* **1**, 33–60

CBA 1982 *Guidelines for the Preparation of Contracts for Archaeological Excavations.* London: Council for British Archaeology

Challis, K and Howard, A J 2006 'A Review of trends within archaeological remote sensing in alluvial environments'. *Archaeol Prospection* **13**, 231–40

Cheetham, P 2005 'Forensic Geophysical Survey' *in* Hunter, J. and Cox, M. (eds), *Forensic archaeology: advances in theory and practice,* London: Routledge, 62–95

Chwala, A, Ijsselsteijn, R, May, T, Oukhanski, N, Schüler, T, Schultze, V, Stolz, R and Meyer, H-G 2003 'Archaeometric prospection with High-T_C SQUID gradiometers'. *IEEE Trans Applied Superconductivity* **13**, 767–70

Chwala, A, Stolz, R, Ijsselsteijn, R, Schultze, V, Ukhansky, N, Meyer, H-G and Schüler, T 2001 'SQUID gradiometers for archaeometry'. *Superconductor Sci Technol* **14**, 1111–14

Ciminale, M and Loddo, M 2001 'Aspects of magnetic data processing'. *Archaeol Prospection* **8**, 239–46

Clark, A J 1983 'The testimony of the topsoil', *in* G S Maxwell (ed.), *The Impact of Aerial Reconnaissance on Archaeology.* London: CBA Res Rep **9**, 128–35

Clark, A J and Haddon-Reece, D 1972–3 'An automatic recording system using a Plessey fluxgate gradiometer'. *Prospezioni Archeol* **7–8**, 107–13

Clark, A J 1992 'Archaeogeophysical prospecting on alluvium', *in* S Needham and M G Macklin (eds), *Alluvial Archaeology in Britain.* Oxbow Monogr **27**. Oxford: Oxbow

Clark, A J C 1996 *Seeing Beneath the Soil* 2nd edn. London: Batsford

Clarke, C M, Utsi, E and Utsi, V 1999 'Ground penetrating radar investigations at North Ballachulish Moss, Highland Scotland'. *Archaeol Prospection* **6**, 107–21

Cole, M A, Linford, N T, Payne, A P and Linford, P K 8–10 September 1995 'Soil magnetic susceptibility measurements and their application to archaeological site investigation', *in* J Beavis and K Barker (eds), *Science and Site: Evaluation and Conservation, Proceedings of the Conference Held 8-10 September 1993* Bournemouth: Bournemouth University Occas Pap **1**, 114–62

Collier, L, Hobbs, B, Neighbour, T and Strachan, R 2003 'Resistivity imaging survey of Capo Long Barrow, Aberdeenshire'. *Scottish Archaeological Internet Report* **6** www.sair.org.uk/sair6/index.html [visited 26/02/2008]

Conyers, L B 2004 *Ground Penetrating Radar for Archaeology*. Walnut Creek, CA: AltaMira Press

Conyers, L B 2012 *Interpreting ground-penetrating radar for archaeology,* Walnut Creek, Calif.: Left Coast Press.

Conyers, L B and Goodman, D 1997 *Ground Penetrating Radar: An Introduction for Archaeologists*. Walnut Creek, CA: AltaMira Press

Council of Europe 1992 'European Convention on the Protection of the Archaeological Heritage (Revised)', [online], available: http://conventions.coe.int/Treaty/en/Treaties/Html/143.htm accessed 28 Jan 2014].

Cox, C 1992 'Satellite imagery, aerial photography and wetland archaeology – an interim report on an application of remote sensing to wetland archaeology: the pilot study in Cumbria, England'. *World Archaeol* **24**, 249–67

Dabas, M 2006 'La prospection géophysique' *in* Dabas, M., Delétang, H., Alain Ferdière, Jung, C. and Zimmermann., W. H. (eds), *La prospection*, Paris: Édition Errance, 167–216

Dabas, M 2009 'Theory and practice of the new fast electrical imaging system ARP©' *in* Campana, S. and Piro, S. (eds), *Seeing the Unseen. Geophysics and Landscape Archaeology*, London: Taylor & Francis Group, 105–126

Dabas, M, Hesse, A and Tabbagh, J 2000 'Experimental resistivity survey at Wroxeter archaeological site with a fast and light recording device'. *Archaeol Prospection* **7**, 107–18

Dalan, R A and Banerjee, S K 1996 'Soil magnetism, an approach for examining archaeological landscapes'. *Geophys Res Letters* **23**, 185–8

Dalan, R A and Banerjee, S K 1998 'Solving archaeological problems using techniques of soil magnetism'. *Geoarchol* **13**, 3–36

Daniels, D (ed.) 2004 *Ground Penetrating Radar*. London: IEE

Darvill, T 1993 'Working practices', *in* J Hunter and I Ralston (eds), *Archaeological Resource Management in the UK: an Introduction*. Stroud: Alan Sutton, 169–83

Darvill, T and Atkins, M 1991 *Regulating Archaeological Work by Contract*. IfA Technical Pap **8**. Birmingham: Institute of Field Archaeologists

David, A 1994 'The role of geophysical survey in early medieval archaeology'. *Anglo-Saxon Studies in Archaeology and History* **7**

Davis, J C and Sampson, R J 1986 *Statistics and Data Analysis in Geology* 2 edn. Chichester: Wiley

Dearing, J A, Hay, K L, Baban, S M J, Huddleston, A S, Wellington, E M H and Loveland, P J 1996 'Magnetic susceptibility of soil: an evaluation of conflicting theories using a national data-set'. *Geophys J Internat* **127**, 728–34

De Smedt, P, Saey, T, Lehouck, A, Stichelbaut, B, Meerschman, E, Islam, M M, Van De Vijver, E and Van Meirvenne, M 2013a 'Exploring the potential of multi-receiver EMI survey for geoarchaeological prospection: A 90ha dataset', *Geoderma*, **199**, 30–36

De Smedt, P, Van Meirvenne, M, Herremans, D, De Reu, J, Saey, T, Meerschman, E, Crombe, P and De Clercq, W 2013b 'The 3-D reconstruction of medieval wetland reclamation through electromagnetic induction survey', *Scientific Reports,* **3**, 1517.

Department for Communities and Local Government 2012 *National Planning Policy Framework*, London: Department for Communities and Local Government.

Di Filippo, M, Ruspandini, T and Toro, B 2000 'The role of gravity surveys in archaeology', *in* M Pasquinucci and F Trément (eds), *Non-Destructive Techniques Applied to Landscape Archaeology*. Archaeology of Mediterranean Landscapes **4**. Oxford: Oxbow, 148–54

Donoghue, D N M and Shennan, I 1988 'The application of multi-spectral remote sensing techniques to wetland archaeology', *in* P Murphy and C French (eds), *The Exploitation of Wetlands*. BAR, Brit Ser **186**, 47–59

Drahor, M G 2004 'Application of the self-potential method to archaeological prospection: some case studies'. *Archaeol Prospection* **11**, 77–105

Drahor, M G, Kurtulmus, T Ö, Berge, M A, Hartmann, M and Speidel, M A 2008 'Magnetic imaging and electrical resistivity tomography studies in a Roman military installation found in Satala archaeological site, northeastern Anatolia, Turkey', *Journal of Archaeological Science,* **35**(2), 259–271

Eder-Hinterleitner, A, Neubauer, W and Melichar, P 1996 'Restoring magnetic anomalies'. *Archaeol Prospection* **3**, 185–98

English Heritage 2002 *With Alidade and Tape: graphical and plane table survey of archaeological earthworks*. Swindon: English Heritage

English Heritage 2003 *Where on Earth are We? The Global Positioning System (GPS) in archaeological field survey*. Swindon: English Heritage

English Heritage 2006 *Our Portable Past: a statement of English Heritage policy and good practice for portable antiquities/surface collected material in the context of field archaeology and survey programmes (including the use of metal detectors)*. Swindon: English Heritage

English Heritage 2007 *Geoarchaeology: using earth sciences to understand the archaeological record*. Swindon: English Heritage

English Heritage 2008 *Geophysical Survey in Archaeological Field Evaluation*, 2nd ed., Swindon: English Heritage.

Eppelbaum, L V, Khesin, B E and Itkis, S E 2001 'Prompt magnetic investigations of archaeological remains in areas of infrastructure development: Israeli experience'. *Archaeol Prospection* **8**, 163–86

European Commission 1999 *Radio and telecommunications terminal equipment (R&TTE) directive 1999/5/EC*, Brussels: European Commission.

Evans, M E and Heller, F 2003 *Environmental Magnetism Principles and Applications of Enviromagnetics*. San Diego: Academic Press

Fajklewicz, Z J 1976 'Gravity vertical measurements for the detection of small geologic and anthropogenic forms'. *Geophysics* **41**, 1016–30

Fassbinder, J W E 2009 'Geophysikalische Prospektionsmethoden - Chancen für das archäologische Erbe, in Tocare - Non Tocare' *in* Emmerling, E. (ed.), München: Siegl, 10–32

Fassbinder, J W E and Irlinger, W E 1994 'Aerial and magnetic prospection of an eleventh to thirteenth century motte in Bavaria', *Archaeological Prospection,* **1**(1), 65–69

Fassbinder, J W E and Stanjek, H 1993 'Occurrence of bacterial magnetite in soils from archaeological sites'. *Archaeol Polona* **31**, 117–28

Fassbinder, J W E, Stanjek, H and Vali, H 1990 'Occurrence of magnetic bacteria in soil', *Nature,* **343**, 161–163

Flageul, S, Dabas, M, Thiesson, J, Rejiba, F and Tabbagh, A 2013 'First in situ tests of a new electrostatic resistivity meter', *Near Surface Geophysics,* **11**(3), 265–273

Foley, J D, van Dam, A, Feiner, S K and Hughes, J F 1991 *Computer Graphics: Principles and Practice* 2 edn. Wokingham: Addison Wesley

Frazier, C H, Cadalli, N, Munson, D C and O'Brien, W D 2000 'Acoustic imaging of objects in soil'. *J Acoustic Soc America* **108**, 147–56

Gaffney, C, Gaffney, V, Neubauer, W, Baldwin, E, Chapman, H, Garwood, P, Moulden, H, Sparrow, T, Bates, R, Löcker, K, Hinterleitner, A, Trinks, I, Nau, E, Zitz, T, Floery, S, Verhoeven, G and Doneus, M 2012 'The Stonehenge Hidden Landscapes Project', *Archaeological Prospection,* **19**(2), 147–155

Gaffney, C and Gater, J A 1993 'Practice and method in the application of geophysical techniques in archaeology', *in* J Hunter and I Ralston (eds), *Archaeological Resource Management in the UK: An Introduction.* Stroud: Alan Sutton, 205–14

Gaffney, C and Gater, J 2003 *Revealing the Buried Past: Geophysics for Archaeologists,* Strout: Tempus Publishing Ltd.

Gaffney, C F, Gater, J A, Linford, P, Gaffney, V L and White, R 2000 'Large-scale systematic fluxgate gradiometry at the roman city of Wroxeter', *Archaeological Prospection,* **7**(2), 81–99

Gaffney, C, Gater, J A and Ovenden, S M 2002 *The Use of Geophysical Techniques in Archaeological Evaluations.* IfA Technical Pap **6**. Reading: Institute of Field Archaeologists

Gebbers, R, Lück, E, Dabas, M and Domsch, H 2009 'Comparison of instruments for geoelectrical soil mapping at the field scale', *Near Surface Geophysics,* **7**(3), 179–190

Glover, J M 1987 'The use of sub-surface radar for shallow site investigation'. London: Kings College, University of London PhD thesis

Goodman, D, Nishimura, Y, Hongo, H and Higashi, N 2006 'Correcting for topography and the tilt of ground-penetrating radar antennae'. *Archaeol Prospection* **13**, 157–61

Goulty, N R, Gibson, J P C, Moore, J G and Welfare, H 1990 'Delineation of the vallum at Vindobala, Hadrian's Wall, by shear-wave seismic refraction survey'. *Archaeometry* **32**, 71–82

Haigh, J G B 1992 'Automatic grid balancing in geophysical survey', *in* G Lock and J Moffett (eds), *Computer Applications and Quantative Methods in Archaeology 1991.* BAR **S577**, 191–6

Heron, C 2001 'Geochemical prospecting', *in* D R Brothwell and A M Pollard (eds), *Handbook of Archaeological Sciences.* Chichester: Wiley, 565–73

Hildebrand, J A, Wiggins, S M, Henkart, P C and Conyers, L B 2002 'Comparison of seismic reflection and ground-penetrating radar imaging at the Controlled Archaeological Test Site, Champaign, Illinois'. *Archaeol Prospection* **9**, 9–21

Howard, A J and Macklin, M G 1999 'A generic geomorphological approach to archaeological interpretation and prospection in British river valleys: a guide for archaeologists investigating Holocene landscapes'. *Antiquity* **73**, 527–41

Huang, H and Won, I J 2000 'Conductivity and susceptibility mapping using broadband electromagnetic sensors'. *J Environm Engineering Geophy* **5**, 31–41

ICOMOS 1990 'Charter for the Protection and Management of the Archaeological Heritage', [online], available: http://www.international.icomos.org/charters/arch_e.pdf [accessed 28 Jan 2014].

IfA 2008 *Standard and Guidance for Archaeological Field Evaluation 3 edn*. Reading: IfA

IfA 2011 *Standard and Guidance for Archaeological Geophysical Survey*. Reading: IfA

Jol, H and Bristow, C 2003 'GPR in sediments: advice on data collection, basic processing and interpretation, a good practice guide', *in* C Bristow and H Jol (eds), *Ground Penetrating Radar in Sediments*. London: Geological Society Special Pub **211**

Jorgensen, M S 1997 'Looking into the landscape'. *Aarhus Geoscience* 7, 157–66

Kattenberg, A E and Aalbersberg, G 2004 'Archaeological prospection of the Dutch perimarine landscape by means of magnetic methods', *Archaeological Prospection,* **11**(4), 227–235

Keller, G V and Frischknecht, F C 1966 *Electrical Methods in Geophysical Prospecting*. New York: Pergamon

Kooiman, G and de Jongh, I G 1994 'Thermal revelations', *in* J Taylor (ed.), *The Conservation and Repair of Ecclesiastical Buildings*. London: Cathedral Communications, 10–11

Kvamme, K L 2003 'Multidimensional prospecting in North American Great Plains village sites'. *Archaeol Prospection* **10**, 131–42

Leckebusch, J 2003 'Ground penetrating radar: a modern three-dimensional prospection method'. *Archaeol Prospection* **10**, 213–41

Leckebusch, J 2005 'Precision real-time positioning for fast geophysical prospection'. *Archaeol Prospection* **12**, 199–202

Leckebusch, J 2011 'Comparison of a stepped-frequency continuous wave and a pulsed GPR system', *Archaeological Prospection,* **18**(1), 15–25

Leckebusch, J and Rychener, J 2007 'Verification and topographic correction of GPR data in three dimensions'. *Near Surface Geophysics* **5**, 395–403

Lee, E 2006 *Management of Research Projects in the Historic Environment – The MoRPHE Project Managers Guide*. Swindon: English Heritage

Leech, C and Hill, I 2008 'Development of a multi-sensor exploration equipment platform for shallow geophysical applications', *First Break,* **26**(3), 113–120

Lehmann, F and Green, A G 1999 'Semiautomated georadar data acquisition in three dimensions'. *Geophysics* **64**, 719–31

Linford, N T 1998 'Geophysical survey at Boden Vean, Cornwall, including an assessment of the microgravity technique for the location of suspected archaeological void features'. *Archaeometr,* **40**, 187–216

Linford, N 2003 'Magnetic Susceptibility', *in* M Brennand and M Taylor (eds), *The Survey and Excavation of a Bronze Age Timber Circle at Holme-next-the-Sea, Norfolk, 1998–9). Proceed Prehist Soc* **69**, 1–84

Linford, N 2004 'From hypocaust to hyperbola: ground penetrating radar surveys over mainly Roman remains in the UK'. *Archaeol Prospection* **11**, 237–46

Linford, N T 2004 'Magnetic ghosts: mineral magnetic measurements on Roman and Anglo-Saxon graves', *Archaeological Prospection,* **11**(3), 167–180

Linford, N 2005 'Archaeological applications of naturally occurring nanomagnets'. International Conference on Fine Particle Magnetism, 20–22 September 2004, London. *J Physics: Conference Ser* **17**, 127–44

Linford, N 2006 'The application of geophysical methods to archaeological prospection'. *Reports on Progress in Physics* **69**, 2205–57

Linford, P and Welch, C M 2004 'Archaeomagnetic analysis of glassmaking sites at Bagot's Park in Staffordshire, England'. *Physics of the Earth and Planetary Interiors* **147**, 209–21

Linford, N, Linford, P, Martin, L and Payne, A 2007 'Recent results from the English Heritage caesium magnetometer system in comparison to recent fluxgate gradiometers'. *Archaeol Prospection* **14**, 151–66

Linford, N, Linford, P, Martin, L and Payne, A 2010 'Stepped frequency ground-penetrating radar survey with a multi-element array antenna: Results from field application on archaeological sites', *Archaeological Prospection,* **17**(3), 187–198

Linnington, R E 1966 'The test use of a gravimeter on Etruscan chambered tombs at Cerveteri'. *Prospezioni Archeol* **1**, 37–41

Loke, M H 2004 'Tutorial: 2-D and 3-D electrical imaging surveys' . www.geoelectrical.com/coursenotes.pdf [Accessed 13/06/2007]

Loke, M H and Barker, R D 1996 'Practical techniques for 3D resistivity surveys and data inversion'. *Geophys Prospection* **44**, 499–523

Masini, N and Lasaponara, R 2007 'Investigating the spectral capability of QuickBird data to detect archaeological remains buried under vegetated and not vegetated areas', *Journal of Cultural Heritage,* **8**(1), 53–60

Metwaly, M, Green, A G, Horstmeyer, H, Maurer, H, Abbas, A M and Hassaneen, A G 2005 'Combined seismic tomographic and ultrashallow seismic reflection study of an early dynastic Mastaba, Saqqara, Egypt'. *Archaeol Prospection* **12**, 245–56

Milsom, J 2002 *Field Geophysics*. Chichester: Wiley

Moskowitz, B M 1995 'Fundamental units and conversion factors', *in* T J Ahrens (ed.), *Global Earth Geophysics: A Handbook of Physical Constants*. AGU reference shelf **1**. Washington: American Geophysical Union

Needham, S and Macklin, M G 1992 *Alluvial Archaeology in Britain*. Oxford: Oxbow

Neubauer, W, Doneus, M, Trinks, I, Verhoeven, G, Joanna, J, Hinterleitner, A, Seren, S and Löcker, K 2012 'Long-term Integrated Archaeological Prospection at the Roman Town of Carnuntum/Austria' *in* Millett, P. J. u. M. (ed.) *Archaeological Survey and the City*, Oxford: Oxbow, 202–221.

Neubauer, W and Eder-Hinterleitner, A 1998 '3D-interpretation of postprocessed archaeological magnetic prospection data'. *Archaeol Prospection* **4**, 191–205

Neubauer, W, Eder-Hinterleitner, A, Seren, S and Melichar, P 2002 'Georadar in the Roman civil town Carnumtum, Austria: an approach for archaeological interpretation of GPR data'. *Archaeol Prospection* **9**, 135–56

Ovenden, S M 1994 'Applications of seismic refraction to archaeological prospecting'. *Archaeol Prospection* **1**, 53–64

Papadopoulos, N G, Tsourlos, P, Tsokas, G N and Sarris, A 2006 'Two-dimensional and three-dimensional resistivity imaging in archaeological site investigation', *Archaeological Prospection,* **13**(3), 163–181

Papadopoulos, N G, Tsourlos, P, Tsokas, G N and Sarris, A 2007 'Efficient ERT measuring and inversion strategies for 3D imaging of buried antiquities', *Near Surface Geophysics,* **5**(6), 349–361

Payne, M A 1981 'SI and Gaussian CGS units, conversions and equations for use in geomagnetism'. *Physics of the Earth and Planetary Interiors* **26**, 10–16

Pipan, M, Baradello, L, Forte, E, Prizzon, A and Finetti, I 1999 '2-D and 3-D processing and interpretation of multi-fold ground penetrating radar data: a case history from an archaeological site'. *J Applied Geophysics* **41**, 271–92

Powlesland, D J, Lyall, J, Hopkinson, D, Donoghue, D N M, Beck, M, Harte, A and Stott, D 2006 'Beneath the sand – remote sensing, archaeology, aggregates and sustainability: a case study from Heslerton, the Vale of Pickering, North Yorkshire, UK'. *Archaeol Prospection* **13**, 291–9

Reynolds, J M 1997 *An Introduction to Applied and Environmental Geophysics*, Chichester: Wiley

Ruffell, A and Wilson, J 1998 'Near-surface investigation of ground chemistry using radiometric measurements and spectral *gamma*-ray data'. *Archaeol Prospection* **5**, 203–15

Saey, T, Islam, M M, De Smedt, P, Meerschman, E, Van De Vijver, E, Lehouck, A and Van Meirvenne, M 2012 'Using a multi-receiver survey of apparent electrical conductivity to reconstruct a Holocene tidal channel in a polder area', *CATENA*, **95**, 104–111

Schleifer, N, Weller, A, Schneider, S and Junge, A 2002 'Investigation of a Bronze Age plankway by spectral induced polarization', *Archaeological Prospection*, **9**(4), 243–253

Schmidt, A 2001 *Geophysical Data in Archaeology: A Guide to Good Practice,* [online], available: http://ads.ahds.ac.uk/project/goodguides/geophys/ [accessed 20/7/2014]

Schmidt, A 2013a *Earth resistance for archaeologists, Geophysical methods for archaeology,* Lanham: AltaMira Press

Schmidt, A 2013b *Geophysical Data in Archaeology: A Guide to Good Practice,* 2nd, fully revised print ed., Oxford and Oakville: Oxbow Books.

Schmidt, A and Marshall, A 1997 'Impact of resolution on the interpretation of archaeological prospection data' *in* Sinclair, A., Slater, E. and Gowlett, J. (eds), *Archaeological Sciences 1995*, Oxford: Oxbow Books, 343–348

Schmidt, A and Tsetskhladze, G 2013 'Raster was Yesterday: Using Vector Engines to Process Geophysical Data', *Archaeological Prospection,* **20**(1), 59–65

Schultze, V, Chwala, A, Stolz, R, Schulz, M, Linzen, S, Meyer, H-G and Schüler, T 2007 'A superconducting quantum interference device system for geomagnetic archaeometry', *Archaeological Prospection,* **14**(3), 226–229

Schultze, V, Linzen, S, Schüler, T, Chwala, A, Stolz, R, Schulz, M and Meyer, H-G 2008 'Rapid and sensitive magnetometer surveys of large areas using SQUIDs – the measurement system and its application to the Niederzimmern Neolithic double-ring ditch exploration', *Archaeological Prospection,* **15**(2), 113–131

Scollar, I 1962 'Electromagnetic prospecting methods in archaeology'. *Archaeometry* **5**, 146–53

Scollar, I, Tabbagh, A, Hesse, A and Herzog, I (eds) 1990 *Archaeological Prospecting and Remote Sensing*. Topics in Remote Sensing **2**. Cambridge: Cambridge University Press

Sirri, S, Eder-Hinterleitner, A, Melichar, P and Neubauer, W 'Comparison of different GPR systems and antenna configurations at the Roman site of Carnuntum', *in* S Piro (ed.), *6th International Conference on Archaeological Prospection 2005*. Rome: Inst Technologies Applied to Cultural Heritage, 176–80

Somers, L E, Hargrave, M L and Simms, J E 2003 *Geophysical Surveys in Archaeology: Guidance for Surveyors and Sponsors*, ERDC/CERL SR-03-21, Arlington, VA: US Army Corps of Engineers. Engineer Research and Development Center

Somers, L, Linford, N, Penn, W, David, A, Urry, L and Walker, R 2005 'Fixed frequency radio wave imaging of subsurface archaeological features: a minimally invasive technique for studying archaeological sites'. *Archaeometry* **47**, 159–73

Tabbagh, A 1986 'Applications and advantages of the Slingram electromagnetic method for archaeological prospecting'. *Geophysics* **51**, 576–84

Tabbagh, J 2003 'Total field magnetic prospection: are vertical gradiometer measurements preferable to single sensor survey?'. *Archaeol Prospection* **10**, 75–81

Taylor, B N 1995 'Guide for the use of the International System of Units (SI)', *in NIST Guide to SI Units*. National Institute of Standards and Technology Special Pub **811**). Gaithersburg: National Institute of Standards and Technology

Telford, W M, Geldart, L P, Sheriff, R E and Keys, D A 1976 *Applied Geophysics*. Cambridge: Cambridge University Press

Theimer, B D, Nobes, D C and Warmer, B G 1994 'A study of the geo-electrical properties of peatlands and their influence on ground-penetrating radar surveying'. *Geophys Prospecting* **42**, 179–209

Thompson, R and Oldfield, F 1986 *Environmental Magnetism*. London: Allen and Unwin

Tite, M S and Mullins, C E 1969 'Electromagnetic prospecting, a preliminary investigation'. *Prospezioni Archeol* **4**, 95–102

Tite, M S and Mullins, C E 1973 'Magnetic viscosity, quadrature susceptibility and multi-frequency dependence of susceptibility in single domain assemblies of magnetite and maghemite'. *J Geophys Res* **78**, 804–9

Trinks, I, Johansson, B, Gustafsson, J, Emilsson, J, Friborg, J, Gustafsson, C, Nissen, J and Hinterleitner, A 2010 'Efficient, large-scale archaeological prospection using a true three-dimensional ground-penetrating Radar Array system', *Archaeological Prospection,* **17**(3), 175–186

Utsi, E 2001. 'The investigation of a peat moss using ground probing radar', *in* S Vertrella, O Bucci, C Elachi, C Lin, M Rouzé and M Sato (eds), *Remote Sensing by Low Frequency Radars Workshop 2001*. Naples: European Association of Remote Sensing Laboratories

Vafidis, A, Manakou, M, Kritikakis, G, Voganatsis, D, Sarris, A and Kalpaxis, T 2003 'Mapping the ancient port at the archaeological site of Itanos (Greece) using shallow seismic methods'. *Archaeol Prospection* **10**, 163–73

Vaughan, C J 1986 'Ground-penetrating radar surveys used in archaeological investigations'. *Geophysics* **51**, 595–604

Verhegge, J, Missiaen, T and Crombe, P 2012 'Preliminary results of an archaeological survey of the land-sea transition at Doelpolder Noord (prov. of Antwerp, B)', *Notae Praehistoricae,* **32**, 165–174

Wait, J R 1955 'Mutual electromagnetic coupling of loops over a homogeneous ground'. *Geophysics* **20**, 630–8

Walker, A R 1991 *Resistance Meter RM15 Manual version 1.2*. Geoscan Research

Walker, A R 2005 *Geoplot Version 3.00 for Windows: Instruction Manual. Version 1.97*. Geoscan Research

Weston, D 2001 'Alluvium and geophysical prospection'. *Archaeol Prospection* **8**, 265–72

Wiseman, J R and El-Baz, F, (eds) 2007 *Remote sensing in archaeology,* New York: Springer.

Wynn, J C and Sherwood, S I 1984 'The self-potential (SP) method: an inexpensive reconnaissance and archaeological mapping tool'. *J Field Archaeol* **11**, 195–204

Zakosarenko, V, Chwala, A, Ramos, J, Stolz, R, Schultze, V, Lütjen, H, Blume, J, Schüler, T and Meyer, H-G 2001 'HTS dc SQUID systems for geophysical prospection'. *IEEE Trans Applied Superconductivity* **11**, 896–9

PART VI: APPENDICES

1. GLOSSARY

area survey: the gathering of geophysical data over an area, usually across a pre-defined **survey grid**, resulting in a two-dimensional plan image of the results – the term thus excludes isolated survey transects.

alkali-vapour magnetometer: a type of magnetometer capable of making very sensitive measurements of a magnetic field by observing changes in the quantum energy states of electrons exposed to it. The method employed is most readily applied to alkali metals in the gaseous state, as these chemical elements have a single unpaired electron in their outer shell. Also known as optically pumped magnetometers. The most commonly used alkali element is Caesium (see Part IV, 1.2).

appraisal: a rapid reconnaissance of site and records to identify (within the planning framework) whether a development proposal has a potential archaeological dimension requiring further clarification (IfA 2008).

brief: an outline framework of the archaeological circumstances that have to be addressed, together with an indication of the scope of works that will be required.

brownfield: any land that has been previously developed.

caesium magnetometer: currently the most common type of **alkali-vapour magnetometer**.

centre frequency: a nominal value for a GPR antenna describing the dominant operating frequency that will influence the depth of penetration and resolution (see Part IV, 1.4.2).

conductivity (σ): the ability of a material to carry an electric current measured in units of milli-Siemens; also defined as the reciprocal of electrical resistivity.

contact resistance: in an earth resistance survey, the contribution to the total electrical resistance caused by the interface between the electrodes and the soil. It is difficult to make good electrical contact between a temporarily inserted electrode and dry soil, so this is typically the largest contribution to the overall resistance. However, the use of four electrodes and of an earth resistance meter with high internal resistance (impedance) can eliminate most effects from contact resistance (see Part IV, 1.3).

curator: a person or organisation responsible for the conservation and management of archaeological evidence by virtue of official or statutory duties (IfA 2008).

data grid: a square or rectangular block of survey data. Typically an overall area to be surveyed will be divided up into a mosaic of contiguous smaller squares or rectangles, each of which will be methodically covered in turn. When transferred to a computer the data-set from each block is initially stored separately and is termed a data grid. Other names used elsewhere are 'sub-grid' and 'tile'.

digital elevation model (DEM): a topographic model of the bare Earth that can be manipulated by computer programs and stored in a grid format.

digital surface model (DSM): a topographic model of the Earth's surface (including terrain cover such as buildings and vegetation) that can be manipulated by computer programs.

digital terrain model (DTM): a topographic model of the bare Earth that can be manipulated by computer programs.

eddy currents: electrical currents induced in a conductive feature by a changing magnetic field, which in turn produce a secondary electromagnetic field that can be detected by a geophysical instrument.

electrical skin depth: depth to which the alternating electric current induced by an electromagnetic field will extend into a conductive object or soil. This material property is dependent on the frequency of the incident electromagnetic field and the electrical conductivity of the soil. It restricts the depth range of soil conductivity meters when operated at high frequencies over conductive sites.

fiducial (fiduciary) marker: a marker introduced into a sequence of time-triggered measurements that can be related to a fixed position on the ground. The position of each measurement made by a moving instrument can then be deduced by comparing its time-stamp to that of the closest (in time) fiducial markers.

fluxgate magnetometer: a solid-state magnetometer that measures the strength of an ambient magnetic field by observing the effect it has on two oppositely wound solenoids. The solenoids are both magnetised by the same alternating electric current and are placed so close together that, in the absence of any external magnetic field the alternating magnetic fields they generate would cancel each other out (see Part IV, 1.2).

fractional conversion: a ratio of magnetic susceptibility before and after laboratory heating of a soil sample to a maximum possible value. High values may be suggestive of occupation processes (burning) that may otherwise be masked through changes in background geology.

frequency dependence of susceptibility: variation of magnetic susceptibility measured from soil samples in an alternating field at two or more frequencies. High values may indicate the presence of very fine magnetic particles often associated with archaeological settlement activity.

georeferencing: the process of fixing the location of a field survey grid on the surface of the Earth, thus making it possible to re-established it at a later date. This can be achieved by making measurements to landmarks with known positions or by direct co-registration (often using a **GPS/GNSS** system) to a national map coordinate system.

geotechnical survey: any subsurface investigation, geophysical or (semi-) invasive, conducted to assist with the physical rather than archaeological aspects of proposed development or extraction scheme. Such data (e.g. from an auger survey) may also prove useful to archaeological geophysicists.

GPS/GNSS: The Global Navigation Satellite System is a network of satellites that transmit information which is used by small receivers to calculate their own position in world coordinates (WGS84). The first such network, the Global Positioning System (GPS), is operated by the United states while the Globalnaya Navigatsionnaya Sputnikovaya Sistema (GLONASS) is operated by Russia. There are also non-global satellite systems in operation, for example from China.

grid: see **survey grid** and **data grid.**

gradiometer: any instrument that records differences in a measured property between two sensors set at a fixed distance apart, rather than the total value of the property measured using a single sensor. This configuration is usually encountered in magnetometers (see Part IV, 1.2).

grey literature: literature that is produced by all levels of government, academics, business and industry, in print and electronic formats, but which is not distributed by commercial publishers. Most geophysical survey reports fall into this category.

ground-truth: the real physical circumstances that produce the geophysical anomalies measured at the ground surface, usually obtained from direct interventions such as coring, test-pitting, trenching or area excavation. Ground-truth data are used to help validate, calibrate and interpret indirect geophysical and remote sensing responses.

interpolation: a method for calculating values for new data points in between a discrete set of measured data points. Often used to reduce the blocky appearance of greyscale plots of surveys where the field sample density was relatively sparse. Interpolation does not increase the amount of information in a data-set and is *not* a substitute for employing a higher sampling density in the field. Various techniques are available. For data that have very different sampling intervals in the two orthogonal directions advanced techniques, like kriging, may be necessary.

map regression: the process of using historic mapped information (for example old maps from a national mapping agency, tithe and estate maps), working backwards in time from the present day, to investigate and reconstruct the past appearance of sites, buildings and landscapes.

pseudosection: a sequence of earth resistance measurements made along the same surface base-line with different electrode separations and visualised to depict an approximate vertical profile of the variation of apparent electrical resistivity with depth (see Part IV, 1.3.4).

reflector: any object with suitable physical properties to reflect an incident GPR signal, often described as point, planar, dipping, linear, complex (diffuse), *etc.* to indicate the likely nature of the causative feature. Hyperbolic responses can be recorded over reflectors of limited cross-section and show characteristic tails, dependent on the velocity of the radar wave, dipping to either side of an apex immediately above the object.

signal-to-noise ratio: used in a general sense to describe the limit of detection for an individual instrument type or technique where the magnitude of response from an underlying feature is no longer discernible above the background noise level.

specification: a written schedule of works required for a particular project (by a curator, planning archaeologist or client) set out in sufficient detail to be quantifiable, implemented and monitored; normally prepared by or agreed with the relevant curator (IfA 2008).

square array: one possible arrangement of electrodes used for making earth resistance measurements. The four electrodes are positioned at the corners of a square, a configuration particularly suited to four-wheeled cart systems (see Part IV, 1.3).

survey grid: the network of control points used to locate the geophysical survey measurements relative to base mapping and/or absolute position on the Earth's surface (see Part IV, 1.1).

time- (depth-) slices: visual representations extracted from a volume GPR data-set showing successive plan views of the variation of reflector energy from the surface to the deepest recorded response (see Part IV, 1.4.5). Depth slices require time-to-depth conversion of the data and correction for undulating surface topography.

thermoremanent magnetisation: a persistent, permanent, magnetisation acquired by certain magnetic minerals after they have been heated above a threshold temperature and then cooled in an ambient magnetic field (such as the Earth's).

tomography: In the context of geophysics, this term usually describes the process of imaging the subsurface from a sequence of measurements from different directions or configurations. A tomographic algorithm is then used to reconstruct the three-dimensional distribution of material properties from these measurements. Using different electrode configurations to collect electrical resistivity sections over the same area (see Part IV, 1.3.4) can be used for electrical resistivity tomography (ERT). For GPR tomography transmitter and receiver antennas are moved separately on opposite sides of the feature to be investigated (e.g. in boreholes either side of the feature).

travel time: the time required for an incident GPR pulse to pass from the surface to a buried reflector, usually measured in nanoseconds (ns). GPR systems conventionally record the two-way travel time from emission to the reception of the reflection in the receiver antenna. If the electromagnetic ground velocity of the radar wave is known, the distance to the reflector can be calculated (see Part IV, 1.4.2).

twin-probe (twin electrode): an arrangement of electrodes for making earth resistance measurements that is particularly suited to archaeological geophysics. The two current electrodes are each paired with one of the two potential electrodes, one pair is set into the ground at a fixed reference position while the second pair is carried on a mobile frame and inserted into the ground wherever a measurement is to be made (see Part IV, 1.3).

written scheme of investigation (WSI): a detailed scheme for the archaeological evaluation and/or recording of a development site, approved by the Local Authority. In the context of these guidelines. A WSI is equivalent to a **specification** or **project design**.

2. RELATED STANDARDS, CODES AND GUIDANCE

There is currently only one code of practice devoted specifically to data from geophysical survey in archaeology:

- Armin Schmidt 2013 *Geophysical Data in Archaeology: A Guide to Good Practice*. (2nd, fully revised print edition). Oxford and Oakville: Oxbow Books.

Readers should familiarise themselves with:

- Chris Gaffney, John Gater and Susan Ovenden 2002 *The Use of Geophysical Techniques in Archaeological Evaluations*. Reading: IfA Techn Pap **6**.

Codes of practice that otherwise have a bearing on geophysical survey, albeit marginally on its archaeological applications, include:

- Darracott, B W and McCann, D M 1986 *Planning Engineering Geophysical Surveys*. London: Geological Society, Engineering Geology Special Publication Number 2.

- *Engineering Geophysics: Report by the Geological Society Engineering Group Working Party* 1988. *The Quarterly Journal of Engineering Geology* **21** (3). London: The Geological Society.
- Building Research Establishment (BRE) 2002 *Optimising Ground Investigation*. Driscoll: BRE. This digest 'informs building and construction professionals who commission ground investigations, especially clients and their advisors who do not themselves have geotechnical qualifications and experience. It aims to raise awareness of the importance of ground investigation for routine projects and provides a summary of best practice'.

The American Society for Testing and Materials (ASTM: http://www.astm.org/) has produced:

- *ASTM D6429-99 Standard Guide for Selecting Surface Geophysical Methods* (which covers forensic and archaeological applications).
- *ASTM D6429-99 Standard Guide for using the Surface Ground Penetrating radar method for Subsurface Investigation.*

Users of GPR (see Part IV, 1.4) should be aware of, and abide by the European Code of Practice (European Telecommunications Standards Institute (ETSI) Guidance document ETSI EG 202 730 http://bit.ly/1kI85ll, which is based on EuroGPR's Code of Practice http://bit.ly/Rk0rFe). EuroGPR (www.eurogpr.org) is a trade association, open to all GPR practitioners, the goals of which is to promote good practice in the use of GPR for both commercial and academic use throughout Europe, to act as a forum for discussion on topical issues, and to act as a voice for the industry in lobbying European legislative authorities.

Contractual arrangements could follow the *ICE Conditions of Contract for Archaeological Investigation* (2004, Thomas Telford Ltd (www.thomastelford.com)). These are the product of a joint working group of the Institution of Civil Engineers (ICE), the Association of Consulting Engineers (ACE), the Civil Engineering Contractors Association (CECA) and the Institute for Archaeologists (IfA), and regulate the business relationship between the Employer and the specialist Archaeological Contractor.

Familiarity with the following codes and manuals will also be advantageous:

- *Archaeological Investigations Code of Practice for Mineral Operators* 1991. Confederation of British Industry.
- *The British Archaeologists and Developers Liaison Group Code of Practice* 1991.
- ACAO 1993 *Model Briefs and Specifications for Archaeological Assessments and Field Evaluations.*
- Dept of Transport 1993 *Design Manual for Roads and Bridges, Volume 11 Section 3 Part 2: Cultural Heritage.*
- IfA 2008 *Standard and Guidance for Archaeological Field Evaluation 3 edn.* Reading: IfA.

3. EDITORIAL INFORMATION

3.1 CONTRIBUTORS

These guidelines were commissioned by the European Archaeological Council (Europae Archaeologiae Consilium, EAC, http://www.european-archaeological-council.org/) and prepared by Dr Armin Schmidt (GeodataWIZ Ltd, U.K.), Paul Linford (English Heritage, U.K.), Dr Chris Gaffney (University of Bradford, U.K.), Dr Apostolos Sarris (IMS-FORTH Crete, Greece) and Dr Jörg Fassbinder (Bavarian State Heritage Department, Germany). They evolved from the English Heritage guidelines on Geophysical Survey in Archaeological Field Evaluation (English Heritage 2008), written by Dr Andrew David, Dr Neil Linford and Paul Linford (all English Heritage, U.K.) with slightly changed terminology based on other publications (Gaffney and Gater 2003; Schmidt 2013a; Aspinall *et al.* 2008; Schmidt 2013b) and taking a broader European view on the subject. The material in Part IV, 1.7 largely follows Linford (2006) with permission from the Institute of Physics Publishing.

Contributors of images and illustrations used in this text are acknowledged in the figure captions. Where no attribution is provided images and illustrations are courtesy of English Heritage.

3.2 LIST OF PEOPLE CONSULTED

We are indebted to those with whom we have consulted on these guidelines and many of whom have troubled to supply constructive advice and commentaries. These include:

- James Adcock for IfA GeoSIG (GSB Prospection Ltd, U.K.);
- Peter Aherne (U.K.);
- Dave Cowley (Historic Environment Scotland, U.K.);
- Dr Carmen Cuenca-Garcia (IMS-FORTH Crete, Greece);
- Dr Michel Dabas (Geocarta S. A., France);
- Dr Tim Schüler (Thuringian State Department for Cultural Heritage and Archaeology, Germany);
- Dr François-Xavier Simon (IMS-FORTH Crete, Greece);
- Arne Anderson Stamnes (NTNU, Norway);
- Erica Utsi for EuroGPR (Utsi Electronics Ltd, U.K.).

EAC Guidelines 2

Managing Europe's Archaeological heritage

Europae
Archaeologiae
Consilium

EAC Guidelines for the Use of Geophysics in Archaeology: Questions to Ask and Points to Consider

By Armin Schmidt, Paul Linford, Neil Linford, Andrew David, Chris Gaffney, Apostolos Sarris and Jörg Fassbinder

Published by:
Europae Archaeologia Consilium (EAC), Association Internationale sans But Lucratif (AISBL),
Siége social/ Official address
rue des Brigades d'Irlande 1
5100 Namur
BELGIUM
www.e-a-c.org

© The individual authors 2015

The opinions expressed in this volume are those of the individual authors, and do not necessarily represent official policy.

ISBN 978-963-9911-73-4

Brought to publication by Archaeolingua, Hungary
Managing editor: Elizabeth Jerem

Copy editing by Armin Schmidt and Dave Cowley
Layout and cover design by Gergely Hős

Printed by Prime Rate Kft., Hungary
Distribution by Archaeolingua, Hungary

Cover image:
Magnetometer Survey Presented as Colour Contour Plot
Earth Resistance Survey Presented as a Continuous Colour Plot
Dual Sensor Fluxgate Gradiometer Used for Manual Data Collection
Caesium Magnetometer Survey Presented as Greyscale Plot
(All © English Heritage)
SQUID Magnetometer Survey with Towed Sensor Array (© Armin Schmidt)